A COUPLE'S GUIDE
—— TO A ——
GROWING
MARRIAGE

A COUPLE'S GUIDE

—— TO A ——

GROWING

MARRIAGE

GARY CHAPMAN

MOODY PUBLISHERS
CHICAGO

© 2006 by

Gary D. Chapman

Originally published as *Building Relationships: A Discipleship Guide for Married Couples*
©1995 Gary Chapman
LifeWay Press

All Scripture quotations, unless otherwise indicated, are taken from the Holy Bible, New International Version,® NIV.® Copyright © 1973, 1978, 1984 by International Bible Society. Used by permission of Zondervan Publishing House. All rights reserved.

Scripture quotations marked KJV are taken from the King James Version.

ISBN: 0-8024-7299-0
ISBN 13: 978-0-8024-7299-1

Cover Design: Smartt Guys Design
Cover Image: Macduff Everton / Image Bank

We hope you enjoy this book from Moody Publishers. Our goal is to provide high-quality, thought-provoking books and products that connect truth to your real needs and challenges. For more information on other books and products written and produced from a biblical perspective, go to www.moodypublishers.com or write to:

Moody Publishers
820 N. LaSalle Boulevard
Chicago, IL 60610

1 3 5 7 9 10 8 6 4 2

Printed in the United States of America

WELCOME

Table of Contents

Welcome to what may be the most growth-producing experience in your Christian life! *A Couple's Guide to a Growing Marriage* is more than just a study. This course can be a doorway to deeper relationships with God and your spouse. As these two relationships become more intimate, you will grow in self-understanding. As you better understand your emotions, attitudes, needs, and abilities, you will also have a deeper understanding of others. Thus, all of your relationships will be enhanced.

You will learn how to share your life more fully with God, and how to draw on His resources. You will also learn how to share yourself more fully with your spouse:

- How to understand and be understood,
- How to express love,
- How to handle anger, and
- How to resolve conflict.

You will gain insight into your spouse's needs and learn how to meet them. In short, you will discover the "joy potential" in your marriage and your "ministry potential" for God.

In terms of personal spiritual growth, you will gain consistency in:

- Meaningful daily quiet time,
- Weekly life-related Bible study,
- Regular Scripture memory, and
- Productive prayer.

Success will require *discipline* (doing things when you don't feel like doing them), and it will call for *honesty and openness* (the willingness to share with others).

God has never called His people to live in isolation. Adam did not say, "It is not good for the man to be alone" (Genesis 2:18). That was God's analysis. Our deepest sense of fulfillment is found in sharing life with others. Marriage is meant to be the most intimate of all our human relationships.

The sense of closeness,
...of knowing and being known,
...of understanding and being understood,
...of helping and being helped,
is what marriage is all about. Yet for many couples intimacy is only a dream.
A Couple's Guide to a Growing Marriage will help you make the dream a reality.

You will discover the "joy potential" in your marriage.

WHAT IS INVOLVED?

A Couple's Guide to a Growing Marriage requires both private time and shared time. In your private time you will study the Bible, pray, memorize Scripture, and complete learning exercises. The shared time will have two aspects: (1) sharing with your spouse, and (2) sharing with a group of couples. Let's look at each element.

PERSONAL BIBLE STUDY—In your Bible study you will discover God's principles for husband-wife relationships. You will pray and memorize key verses of Scripture that have continuous application to life. Plan to spend one hour each week in personal Bible study. You should complete it the first couple of days in the week because you will apply what you learn in the Bible study during the daily growth exercises.

DAILY GROWTH EXERCISES—The learning exercises you complete as part of your Bible study help you identify your ideas, feelings, and attitudes, and thus develop self-understanding. You will apply what you learn in daily growth exercises. These exercises consist of two aspects: (1) conversations with God, and (2) sharing with your spouse.

Conversations with God—One aspect of daily growth will be conversations with God. This private time consists of 10 to 15 minutes each day. You will grow to value these conversations with God as you spend time talking and listening to Him.

Sharing with Your Spouse—You will learn how to have a brief sharing time (10 to 15 minutes) with your spouse daily. The purpose is for self-revelation and understanding. You will grow closer in your relationship in these times together. Some weeks you will have an extended time by sharing a learning exercise together.

SHARING WITH A GROUP—The group sharing time is one of the most important aspects of *A Couple's Guide to a Growing Marriage*. Interacting with a group provides the encouragement and support needed for consistent growth. You will learn how to share insights from your personal Bible study, and gain the insight of others. You will experience the joy of praying with fellow Christians. You will give and receive encouragement in Scripture memory. You share from your marriage only that which you feel will help others, or those things where you desire the ideas of other couples. You will not be asked to share anything that you do not want to share. The group sharing time will require 1 to 1.5 hours per week. The group will meet at a time and place mutually determined by group members.

WEEKLY FLOW OF ACTIVITIES CHART

SUN	MON	TUES	WED	THURS	FRI	SAT
Conversations with God (every day, 10 to 15 minutes)						
Sharing with Your Spouse (every day, 10 to 15 minutes)						
Group Meeting (1 to 1.5 hours)	Personal Bible Study (1 hour)					

Again, welcome to *A Couple's Guide to a Growing Marriage*, the doorway to deeper relationships with God and your spouse. Your first assignment is chapter 1. You will complete a Bible study, record a prayer request, and perform a learning exercise. Good journey!

— *Gary Chapman*

GROUP LEADERSHIP

If you are the leaders of your group, remember that you are facilitators, not teachers. You are also participants, growing in your relationship with God and with each other. Your task is to facilitate the sharing time and encourage the group members. You may choose to spend additional time outside the group with couples who request such time, but you need not feel you must be authorities on marriage or spiritual growth—you are there as fellow learners.

You will find information on the leader guide that accompanies this study at www.fivelovelanguages.com.

CHAPTER 1

ENHANCING MY CONVERSATION WITH GOD

The fundamental building block in any relationship is conversation—two-way communication. I share my ideas and you listen. You share your ideas and I listen. The results? We understand each other a little better. Continue conversation over a period of time and we get to know each other. The same is true with God. The only way we get to know God is to spend time conversing with Him.

Many Christians have viewed Bible reading and prayer as formal religious exercises. In reality, Bible reading should be equated with listening to God, and prayer is the process of talking and listening to God. Many Christians have also tended to see Bible reading and prayer as two distinct experiences. We read the Bible, close it, and then start praying about things totally unrelated to what we have read. It is as though we say to God, "What You have said is relatively unimportant. Now You listen to what I have to say." All of us have encountered persons who respond to our comments in a similar manner. That is, when we finish speaking, they change the subject and begin telling us something unrelated. Most of us don't care to be around such persons. The greatest insult we can give another person is not to listen when he or she speaks. It is not any different with God.

If you are going to learn effective communication with God, you must join Bible reading and prayer. One way to do that is to mark your Bible as you read and then go back and talk with God about what you marked. Begin your Bible reading with this prayer: "Lord, I will read this chapter from Your Word. I want to hear what You have to say to me. Keep my mind alert and speak to me as I read." Then, with pencil or pen in hand, read the chapter and mark anything that impresses you. Various ways to mark a passage are suggested in the box on this page.

Having read the chapter, go back to those statements that you marked and respond to God.

- You may respond by *asking God a question.* "Lord, is this verse really saying what I think it is saying?" or "Lord, I don't understand. How is this verse related to the verse I read last week on this subject?"
- You may respond to God by *thanking Him for some truth* that you have marked. "Lord, thank You that You do love me with an unending love. That really makes me feel secure. Thank You, Lord."
- You may *respond to God with praise.* "Father, I want to praise You that You are indeed, as this verse says, 'the creator of the ends of the earth.' I praise You as Creator and Sustainer of all life, including me."
- You may want to *respond to God with a request.* "Oh, Lord, I really do want to love

WAYS TO MARK YOUR BIBLE

underline key sentences

circle key words or phrases

* star ideas that seem especially helpful to you

[ ] use brackets around longer passages dealing with same subject

#, ?, ! use other markings that you find helpful

others. Pour Your love in my heart today and show me how to express love to my spouse."

Your responses to God will be as varied as your responses to others. You should express your honest feelings, thoughts, and ideas to God. That is the purpose of communication. God shares His ideas with you and you respond to what He has said.

Having talked with God about the things He has brought to your attention, you are now free to change the subject. You may then talk with God about something unrelated to what you have read. You share with God your concerns, feelings, and desires. Pray for your family, your job, your church, and other concerns.

This two-way process of talking and listening to God should be a daily experience for the Christian. Few things are more important in developing a relationship with God than your personal time with Him each day. Thus, our goal this week is to begin establishing a brief time each day to have an open conversation with God. This will be a regular part of *A Couple's Guide to a Growing Marriage*. Remember from the introduction that this is one aspect of your daily growth exercise. With your Bible and pen, find a quiet place and begin today. We suggest that you read through one book of the Bible before beginning another. If you have not already chosen a book, you may want to begin with Philippians. List the chapter you read each day below.

Monday _____

Tuesday _____

Wednesday _____

Thursday _____

Friday_____

Saturday _____

Sunday _____

BIBLE STUDY

1. Read John 17:3: *"Now this is eternal life: that they may know you, the only true God, and Jesus Christ, whom you have sent."* Write Jesus' definition of eternal life according to this passage. _____
_____
_____

2. Briefly describe how you get to know someone. _____

_____

3. All relationships have a beginning point. When did your relationship with God begin? _____

4. Read Psalm 119:105: *"Your word is a lamp to my feet and a light for my path."* All relationships are enhanced by communication. According to Psalm 119:105, what is God's primary means of communication? His _____

_____

_____

5. Read Psalm 119:9–11: *"How can a young man keep his way pure? By living according to your word. I seek you with all my heart; do not let me stray from your commands. I have hidden your word in my heart that I might not sin against you."* Check some of the results of hearing and obeying God's Word.

❑   Live according to God's Word
❑   Seek God with all my heart
❑   Never have problems
❑   Not sin against God
❑   Not stray from God's commands
❑   Be happy

6. Read Jeremiah 15:16: *"When your words came, I ate them; they were my joy and my heart's delight, for I bear your name, O LORD God Almighty."* According to this passage, what effect did the Word of God have on Jeremiah? _____

_____

_____

What does it mean to "eat" God's Word? _____

_____

7. Read Psalm 119:12–16: *"Praise be to you, O LORD; teach me your decrees. With my lips I recount all the laws that come from your mouth. I rejoice in following your statutes as one rejoices in great riches. I meditate on your precepts and consider your ways. I delight in your decrees; I will not neglect your word."* List several ways found in these

verses in which the psalmist responded to God's Word. _____

_____

_____

8. David said, *"I will not neglect your word"* (Psalm 119:16). What are some of the activities that will help us remember the Word of God?

- ❑   Writing it down
- ❑   Meditating on it
- ❑   Applying it
- ❑   Memorizing it
- ❑   Saying it aloud
- ❑   Discussing it with others

9. Did you list *memorizing* as one method of remembering? In *A Couple's Guide to a Growing Marriage* we will memorize key verses that give us *life principles*, truths that will shape our relationships in marriage. One such verse is, *"Be kind and compassionate to one another"* (Ephesians 4:32).

We will concentrate on learning this portion of this verse this week. At least once a day repeat the reference, the verse, and the reference again. The reference is twice as difficult to remember as the verse. Repeat this sequence now.

> *Ephesians 4:32*
> *Be kind and compassionate to one another.*
> *Ephesians 4:32*

10. Write one way in which you could express kindness to your spouse this week.

_____

(If you cannot think of one, ask your spouse and write the answer above.)
❑   Check here when you have expressed the kindness you noted above.

Note one way in which you were not kind to your spouse during the past few days.

_____

(If you cannot think of one, ask your spouse and write the answer above.)

Your word

is a lamp to

my feet and

a light for

my path.

PSALM 119:105

Not only

does God

talk to us

through

Scripture,

but God

wants us

to talk to

Him about

His Word.

11. Not only does God talk to us through Scripture, but God wants us to talk to Him about His Word. Read Psalm 119:33–40. Match the Scripture passage with the requests David made of God. Write the correct letter on the line beside the reference.

_____v. 33	a. Turn my eyes away from worthless things.
_____v. 34	b. Direct me in the path of your commands.
_____v. 35	c. Preserve my life in your righteousness.
_____v. 36	d. Fulfill your promise to your servant.
_____v. 37	e. Give me understanding.
_____v. 38	f. Turn my heart toward your statutes.
_____v. 39	g. Teach me… to follow your decrees.
_____v. 40	h. Take away the disgrace I dread.

Check your answers below.

12. Read this passage again as a prayer to God emphasizing the words *me, my,* and *mine.* Make it a personal prayer.

(answers to Bible study item 11: g, e, b, f, a, d, h, c)

LEARNING EXERCISE

As you begin *A Couple's Guide to a Growing Marriage,* list three things you would like to see happen in your relationship with God and with your spouse in the next few weeks.

My Relationship with God
Three things I would like to see happen in my relationship with God:
(1) _____
(2) _____
(3) _____

My Relationship with My Spouse
Three things I would like to see happen in my relationship with my spouse:
(1) _____
(2) _____
(3) _____

Include these desires in your personal prayers this week, as you have your daily time of listening to and talking with God.

ENHANCING MY CONVERSATION WITH MY SPOUSE

Last week we talked about getting to know God by means of personal conversation with Him. This week we will discuss getting to know each other as husband and wife by the same process. The Scriptures indicate that husbands and wives are to become "one" (Genesis 2:24). They are to share life to such a degree that they have a sense of unity, or togetherness.

- "We are a team."
- "We know each other."
- "We understand each other."
- "We choose to walk in step with each other."
- "Our lives are inseparably bound together."
- "We are one."

These are the statements of happily married couples.

Becoming "one" does not mean that we have lost our personal identities. We retain our personalities. We have personal goals and ambitions. The typical husband and wife spend many hours each day geographically separated from each other, each pursuing different activities. Marital "oneness" is not sameness, it is rather that inner feeling that assures us that we are "together" even when we are apart. For this to happen, each partner makes the commitment to help the other develop as a person and to reach our potential as an individual and as a couple.

Such "oneness" is not automatic. Becoming "one" is the result of many shared thoughts, feelings, activities, dreams, frustrations, joys, and sorrows. In short, it is the result of sharing life.

Verbal conversation is the primary process by which we share life. All of us know couples who seem to have a genuine sense of "oneness." Unfortunately, most of us know more couples who seem unable to "get it together." The major difference between these two types of couples is that the former has developed consistent communication patterns while the latter has not. One makes time for conversation, while the other simply lets things ride.

Last week we discussed the necessity of establishing a brief time each day for conversation with God. This week we will begin to establish a daily communication time with our spouses. Knowing God is a process that requires regular two-way communication. Knowing and becoming one with your spouse will require the same.

After completing your Bible study, you will find a learning exercise that will help you begin to establish regular communication with your spouse.

BIBLE STUDY

1. Read 1 Corinthians 2:11. *"For who among men knows the thoughts of a man except the man's spirit within him?"* What fact stated in this passage makes communication a necessity in a good marriage? _____

_____

_____

_____

2. If you are the only one who knows your thoughts, why is communication so important in your marriage? _____

_____

_____

_____

_____

3. Read 2 Corinthians 6:11–13: *"We have spoken freely to you, Corinthians, and opened wide our hearts to you. We are not withholding our affection from you, but you are withholding yours from us. As a fair exchange—I speak as to my children—open wide your hearts also."* What is Paul's request of the Corinthians? _____

_____

_____

_____

_____

_____

In what way had Paul set the example for the Corinthians according to these verses?

_____

_____

What may have hindered the Corinthians from opening their hearts and communicating freely with Paul? (This is a thought question, not found in the text.)

_____

_____

Becoming "one" is the result of many shared thoughts, feelings, activities, dreams, frustrations, joys, and sorrows.

He who

answers

before

listening—

that is his

folly and

his shame.

PROVERBS 18:13

What might keep you from opening your heart and sharing freely with your spouse?

_____

_____

4. Read 1 Corinthians 14:8–9: *"Again, if the trumpet does not sound a clear call, who will get ready for battle? So it is with you. Unless you speak intelligible words with your tongue, how will anyone know what you are saying? You will just be speaking into the air."* The context of 1 Corinthians 14:8–9 is guidance for speaking in the church. What principle or guideline might we learn from this passage for communication in marriage? _____

_____

_____

5. Can you think of a recent example in your marriage when you did not speak very clearly, and thus your spouse misunderstood? What problems did that cause in your communication? Briefly describe it here. _____

_____

_____

6. Read James 5:12: *"Let your 'Yes' be yes, and your 'No,' no, or you will be condemned."* What communication principle is found in this verse? _____

_____

_____

Can you give an illustration in your own communication when you said yes but meant no? Briefly describe your illustration. _____

_____

_____

7. Read James 1:19: *"My dear brothers, take note of this: everyone should be quick to listen, slow to speak and slow to become angry."* What three implications for communication are found in this verse?

(a) quick to _____

(b) slow to _____

(c) slow to become _____

What application would the phrase "slow to speak" have for your communication with your spouse? _____

_____

_____

What does the phrase "quick to listen" or "quick to hear" mean to you? _____

_____

_____

8. Read Proverbs 21:13: *"If a man shuts his ears to the cry of the poor, he too will cry out and not be answered."* In what way could the idea of this verse be applied to your listening to your spouse? _____

_____

_____

Read Proverbs 18:13: *"He who answers before listening—that is his folly and his shame."* Paraphrase the truth found in this verse. _____

_____

_____

Can you give an illustration from your marriage when you have answered before hearing? Briefly describe. _____

_____

_____

In terms of basic personality, we tend to think of some persons as "talkers" and others as "listeners." Most of us do lean in one of these directions.

How would you classify yourself? _____

Your spouse? _____

Nothing is wrong with leaning in either direction. However, communication is a two-way street. The listener must learn to open up and share, while the talker must learn to listen genuinely. One of our purposes in the weeks ahead is to help you build better, more effective patterns of communication. The learning exercise that follows is a first step.

LEARNING EXERCISE

1. List below three things that happened in your life today. These may range from the simple act of drinking a cup of coffee, or talking to an old friend, or making a bank deposit, to discovering oil in your backyard.

Three things that happened in my life today:

1. _____
2. _____
3. _____

2. Note below how you feel about each of the three items you listed. In one or more words simply describe how you respond emotionally to each event. You may use such words as *sad, mildly sad, happy, mildly happy, super happy, disappointed, frustrated, angry, fearful,* etc. This is how I feel about the events I listed above.

1. _____
2. _____
3. _____

When you and your spouse have completed numbers 1 and 2 above, sit down and share with each other what you have written. Listen carefully. Ask any questions or make any response you desire. Let him or her do the same as you share. This should take 5 to 10 minutes depending on your responses.

4. Each day this week make time to share with each other "three things that happened in my life today" and "how I feel about them." This process of self-revelation, when done consistently, will set the stage for higher levels of communication. This begins the second aspect of your Daily Growth Exercises that will continue throughout this study.

Check each day this week that you have this "sharing time" with your spouse.

❑ Monday	❑ Friday
❑ Tuesday	❑ Saturday
❑ Wednesday	❑ Sunday
❑ Thursday	

In subsequent chapters, this will be listed in the section Daily Growth Exercises.

SCRIPTURE MEMORY

The purpose of Scripture memorization is not to be able to quote Scripture. Memorization is, rather, to get the truth of Scripture into your life. The process of memorizing imprints the truth in your mind, which is an important step toward applying it to your life. In this course, you will memorize only a few verses, all of which have direct implication for marriage relationships. One such verse is Ephesians 4:32, which you began memorizing last week.

"Be kind and compassionate to one another." (Ephesians 4:32)

Concentrate this week on memorizing the entire verse. You may want to write it on a card and place it where you can read it several times each day. Remember to repeat the reference before and after you repeat the verse. This aids in remembering where the verse is located in the Bible. This will be important later as you share with others. You are welcome to memorize the verse in another translation. At the back of this guide, you will find the verse printed in the New International Version.

 **DAILY GROWTH EXERCISES**

Conversations with God. You will want to continue your personal conversations with God each day. List below the chapters you read and discuss with God each day.

Monday _____

Tuesday _____

Wednesday _____

Thursday _____

Friday _____

Saturday _____

Sunday _____

Be kind and compassionate to one another, forgiving each other, just as in Christ God forgave you.

EPHESIANS 4:32

LEARNING TO FORGIVE

Perfection would be heavenly! I wish that I were a perfect husband: always kind, thoughtful, understanding, considerate, and loving. Unfortunately, I am not. None of us are. I am sometimes selfish, thoughtless, and cold. In short, I fail to live up to the biblical ideal for a Christian husband. Does that mean that my marriage is destined for failure? Not if I am willing to admit my failures and my wife is willing to forgive.

Forgiveness is not simply overlooking the failures of your spouse. God's forgiveness is our model. God forgives us based on what Christ did for us on the cross (see Ephesians 4:32). God does not overlook sin. Christ paid the full penalty for our sin, thus making forgiveness possible. Even then, God does not forgive everyone, but only those who are willing to admit sin and their need of forgiveness. God promises to hold our sins against us no longer, *if* we are willing to confess them (see 1 John 1:9). Genuine confession always precedes true forgiveness.

There is a difference between forgiveness and acceptance. You may accept many things about your spouse that you do not particularly like. In fact, such acceptance is necessary in healthy marriages. But forgiveness presupposes that you have been wronged, treated unfairly or unjustly. In the Bible such action is called sin and sin cannot be accepted. There are two responses to sin: the person lives constantly with the sin, or the person confesses and is forgiven. When we forgive someone, we say: "Since you have admitted your sin, I forgive you. I will no longer hold that against you. I will respond to you as though it had not happened." The challenge in Scripture is to forgive one another "just as in Christ God forgave you" (Ephesians 4:32).

The Bible study and learning exercise this week are designed to help you establish a pattern of dealing realistically with your failures and learning to forgive your spouse.

 **BIBLE STUDY**

1. *"If we confess our sins, he [God] is faithful and just and will forgive us our sins and purify us from all unrighteousness"* (1 John 1:9).
According to this verse, what must we do to experience God's forgiveness? _____
_____

2. What does the word *confess* mean? Check all that apply. You may want to refer to a dictionary.

- ❏ To tell or to make known
- ❏ To acknowledge a wrongdoing
- ❏ To blame or accuse someone
- ❏ To find fault in another person's actions

3. Read Psalm 32:1–5. Briefly describe the experience of David. _____
_____

The Bible provides us a model of forgiveness that far exceeds our comprehension. God's forgiveness offers us insight in how we are to forgive others — especially our marriage partner.

4. *"As far as the east is from the west, so far has he removed our transgressions from us"* (Psalm 103:12). What is the extent of God's forgiveness? Underline your answer in the verse.

5. *"And their sins and lawless acts I will remember no more"* (Hebrews 10:17). In this verse, what do you think is meant by God not remembering our sins?

6. Is there a difference between forgiving and forgetting?

- ❏ Yes
- ❏ No

Explain your answer. _____
_____

7. How would you answer the person who says, "I have forgiven him or her, but I have trouble with my feelings when I remember what he or she did"? _____
_____

Forgiveness does not destroy our memory. Our brains record every event we have experienced. Memory may bring back the feeling of hurt and pain. But forgiveness is not a feeling; it is a promise. Forgiveness is the promise that is reflected in the statement: "I will no longer hold that against you."

God forgives

us based on

what Christ

did for us

on the cross.

Suppose my wife, Karolyn, has confessed a failure and I have chosen to forgive. When memory brings back the pain and hurt, I can take the emotions to God and thank Him that even though I still feel this pain, that sin is now forgiven. I ask Him to help me do something loving for Karolyn today. In time, the memory and the pain will diminish as we build new positive memories together.

8. *"Be kind and compassionate to one another, forgiving each other, just as in Christ God forgave you"* (Ephesians 4:32). According to this verse, who is our model in forgiving? _____

9. First John 1:9 states: *"If we confess our sins, he [God] is faithful and just and will forgive us our sins and purify us from all unrighteousness."*

Summarize the two elements of God's forgiveness as found in 1 John 1:9.

My responsibility: _____

_____

God's response: _____

_____

10. What is the biblical pattern you are to follow when you have sinned against your spouse? Look at Matthew 5:23–24 for your answers: *"Therefore, if you are offering your gift at the altar and there remember that your brother has something against you, leave your gift there in front of the altar. First go and be reconciled to your brother; then come and offer your gift."*

Your responsibility: _____

_____

Responsibility of your spouse: _____

_____

11. What is the biblical pattern you are to follow when your spouse has sinned against you? Look at Matthew 18:15 for your answers: *"If your brother sins against you, go and show him his fault, just between the two of you. If he listens to you, you have won your brother over."*

Your responsibility: _____

_____

Responsibility of your spouse: _____

_____

12. Look again at Ephesians 4:32. What is the relationship between being "tenderhearted" (KJV) and "forgiving each other" (NIV)? _____

_____

13. How many times are we to forgive? Read Jesus' conversation with Peter recorded in Matthew 18:21–22. *"Then Peter came to Jesus and asked, 'Lord, how many times shall I forgive my brother when he sins against me? Up to seven times?' Jesus answered, 'I tell you, not seven times, but seventy-seven times.'"* Circle the number. What are the implications of this verse for us? _____

_____

14. *"For if you forgive men when they sin against you, your heavenly Father will also forgive you. But if you do not forgive men their sins, your Father will not forgive your sins"* (Matthew 6:14–15). What do these verses say to us about the importance of forgiving others? _____

_____

 ## LEARNING EXERCISE

The following exercises will help you apply the principles of confession and forgiveness discovered in your Bible study. The psalmist said,

> *Search me, O God, and know my heart: test me, and know my anxious thoughts: See if there is any offensive way in me, and lead me in the everlasting way.*
> (Psalm 139:23–24)

Put this prayer in your own words and ask God to show you where you are failing your spouse. You know that you are not perfect, but what are your imperfections? What are you failing to do that you should be doing? What are you doing that should not be done? Where are you failing to meet his or her needs? What have you said that is unkind? What have you left unsaid that could have brought encouragement?

After you have asked God to help you identify specific failures, do the following:

1. Write those things that God brings to your mind. Be specific.

2. Having made a list, go back and confess each of these failures to God.

3. After confession, thank God for His forgiveness. Remember that the Scriptures say that if we confess, God will forgive (see 1 John 1:9). Verbal thanks to God is a way to express faith in His promise.

4. In your next sharing time, tell you spouse what you have done and ask permission to share your list. You might say, "These are some areas in which I feel I have failed you. I want to share them and ask you to forgive me." Then, read your list and wait for his or her response. Hopefully, your spouse will express forgiveness. Cross out the list as a symbol of forgiveness.

5. You may want to seal your confession and forgiveness by some act of love: hold hands, embrace, kiss, or look into the eyes of your spouse and say, "I love you."

Your spouse may wish to share his or her list with you at this time, or at a later time. It is important that both of you complete this learning exercise. Write the date you completed this exercise: _____

SCRIPTURE MEMORY

This week, we will continue to learn Ephesians 4:32. One of the keys to memorizing Scripture is to review the verse several times each day. Our purpose is to make the verse a part of life. There is no substitute for review. Take a moment now and quote

Ephesians 4:32. Look and see if you have quoted it correctly. If not, read it agai[n]
work at it until you can say it perfectly. Repeat this process several times each da[y].

> *Be kind and compassionate to one another, forgiving each other, just as in Ch[rist]
> God forgave you. (Ephesians 4:32)*

At least once this week, have your spouse listen as you quote the verse. When y[ou]
quote it perfectly with the reference before and after the verse, record the date of
your accomplishment below.

Ephesians 4:32 was quoted correctly on _____

DAILY GROWTH EXERCISES

Conversations with God. Please indicate on the record sheet (page 129) the chapters
which you *read*, *marked*, and *discussed* with God through this week (week 3). You
may want to fill in weeks 1 and 2 from chapters 1 and 2. You will be using this chart
from now on in this course, and hopefully, after the course as you establish regular
conversations with God. Remember, your objective is to make this time with God a
part of each day.

Sharing Time with My Spouse. Last week you began the process of establishing a
daily sharing time with your spouse. This week, continue sharing three things that
happened in your life each day, and your emotional response to those events. You
may discuss other matters as you wish, but make this a minimum goal for each
day. On page 131 record the days on which you have this sharing time with your
spouse (week 3). The purpose of the record is to help you build consistency in this
important communication pattern.

compassionate

to one another,

forgiving each

other, just as

in Christ God

forgave you.

EPHESIANS 4:32

DEVELOPING MY SERVE

The key that unlocks the door to a happy marriage is learning to serve your spouse! If we are honest, most of us would admit that we entered marriage with lofty visions of what our spouses would do for us. When they did not perform as we had envisioned, we were disappointed, hurt, angry, and maybe even hostile. We made verbal demands and then made them feel guilty when they did not respond to our demands. "I don't understand how you could do that. You know how it makes me feel." "Why don't you do this? You know how important it is to me." With such statements, we try to manipulate their behavior. We try to get what we want. In short, we try to "lord it over" our marriage partners, the very thing Jesus condemned (see Mark 10:42).

In a good marriage, there is no king or queen shouting commands, only servants looking for ways to meet the needs of others. Jesus said that the road to greatness is the road of service (see Mark 10:43). History illustrates this truth. The truly great men and women of any age are those who serve others. The greatest political leaders have made the greatest contributions to their constituents. The truly great physicians have given unselfishly for the benefit of their patients. Religious leaders come and go, but those who make a lasting impact are those who have learned how to serve people. Great sermons will be forgotten, but acts of service speak forever. Thus, the greatest husbands are the greatest servants. The wife who finds greatest fulfillment is the wife who learns to serve.

For some people, it takes a radical change of attitude for them to become a servant. Our society has trained us in assertiveness, not service. Servanthood may not be a favorite topic for seminars, though it ought to be, for servanthood is the only road to greatness. Your Bible study and learning exercise this week will challenge you to a new way of thinking. If you respond positively, you may find that this week will open up a new world of greatness for you.

A mutual attitude of service on the part of both husband and wife leads to needs being met. This attitude must be mutual. A submitting, serving wife and a tyrannical, demanding husband will never produce a happy marriage. A domineering wife and a passive husband will also fail to find marital fulfillment. The husband must learn to serve his wife as Christ served the church (see Ephesians 5:25). The wife must serve her husband "as to the Lord" (Ephesians 5:22). Mutual service brings mutual joy.

Few weeks are more important than this week in *A Couple's Guide to to a Growing Marriage.* Developing your serve could make the difference between success and failure in your marriage. Tennis players spend hours each week improving their serves. Should you give less to improving the one aspect of your marriage that has the potential for making your marriage great?

 **BIBLE STUDY**

1. Read Mark 10:35–45. How would you characterize the attitude of James and John? _____
_____

Look closely at verse 42: *"Jesus called them together and said, 'You know that those who are regarded as rulers of the Gentiles lord it over them, and their high officials exercise authority over them'"* (Mark 10:42). How did Jesus describe the non-Christian's view of leadership? _____
_____

In contrast, what is to be the Christian's attitude? Circle phrases in Mark 10:43–44 that answer this question: *"Not so with you. Instead, whoever wants to become great among you must be your servant, and whoever wants to be first must be slave of all."*
_____
_____

According to Mark 10:45, what was Christ's purpose in coming? *"For even the Son of Man did not come to be served, but to serve, and to give his life as a ransom for many."*
_____
_____
_____

In your own words, summarize the teaching of Mark 10:42–45. _____
_____
_____

Clearly, Jesus affirmed the servant role of His disciples and challenged them to be like Him by being a servant to all. As His followers today, we are to do the same. Let's consider one of Jesus' best examples of service to others.

2. Read John 13:1–17. In what way did Jesus serve the disciples? _____
_____
_____

For even the Son of Man did not come to be served, but to serve, and to give his life as a ransom for many.

MARK 10:45

In our day, what would compare to foot washing in Jesus' day? Add your answers to the following list.

- Taking out the trash
- Making dinner
- _____
- _____

Jesus summarized the lesson in verses 12–17. In your own words, what was Jesus teaching? _____
_____

Verse 17 says: *"Now that you know these things, you will be blessed if you do them."* What truth does this verse emphasize? Check one:

- ❏ God affirms acts of service to others.
- ❏ Knowing what to do is as good as doing it.
- ❏ Material gain comes to those who serve others.

Jesus' example is a powerful one for us to follow. It is reaffirmed by other New Testament writers that recognized the place of servanthood in the Christian's life.

3. Read Philippians 2:1–8 in at least two translations. Whose example are we to follow?

- ❏ Christ
- ❏ Good people
- ❏ Other Christians
- ❏ Great teachers

Summarize the attitude of Christ by circling one word in verse 7 that expresses that attitude:

But made himself nothing, taking the very nature of a servant, being made in human likeness.

Read verses 7 and 8 again. How did Christ demonstrate His servanthood? _____
_____
_____

Do nothing out of selfish ambition or vain conceit, but in humility consider others better than yourselves.

PHILIPPIANS 2:3

The attitude of servanthood is explained in verses 3–4. Underline what we are told to do.

> *Do nothing out of selfish ambition or vain conceit, but in humility consider others better than yourselves. Each of you should look not only to your own interests, but also to the interests of others.*

4. Esteeming or counting someone as being more important than ourselves is the opposite of what we normally do. When you apply this principle to the way you think and act toward your spouse, what are some actions you would demonstrate?

_____

_____

_____

5. *"Serve one another in love. The entire law is summed up in a single command: 'Love your neighbor as yourself.' If you keep on biting and devouring each other, watch out or you will be destroyed by each other"* (Galatians 5:13–15). In this passage Paul gives a challenge and a warning concerning our love and service to others. Put these in your own words.

Paul's challenge: _____

_____

_____

Paul's warning: _____

_____

_____

6. Developing your serve is not easy, but it is rewarding. Consider again John 13:17 and fill in the blank that states the results of serving others. *"Now that you know these things, you will be _____ if you do them."*

LEARNING EXERCISE

Happiness is something all couples want, but few achieve. Those who do achieve happiness have discovered the secret. You can too. Happiness is the result of serving, not of demanding. This exercise will help you develop your serve.

1. List the ways you served your spouse yesterday. Include the entire day from the time you awakened until you went to sleep. Be as specific as you can and include every act of service, large or small. For example: prepared her breakfast, picked up his dry cleaning. _____

_____

_____

_____

2. Make a list of several things you know that your spouse would like you to do for him or her. These may include regular activities like taking out the garbage, or occasional projects such as painting the bedroom. At this stage in the exercise, don't ask your partner what should be on this list. That will come later. _____

_____

_____

_____

3. The items you just listed provide a good source of ideas on how you can serve your spouse. Choose one you will do or begin to do today.

Act of service for my spouse: _____

_____

_____

Date completed: _____

4. Complete at least two other acts of service for your spouse this week. These need not be large or time-consuming, but they need to be acts you consciously do in a spirit of service to your spouse. Record them and the date you complete each one.

Act of service for my spouse: _____

_____

Date completed: _____

Act of service for my spouse: _____
_____

Date completed: _____

5. When you and your spouse have completed steps 1–4 above, share your answers with each other. If you feel comfortable doing so, ask your mate to help you build your list of things he would like you to do for him. This will help you identify practical ways to express your growing attitude of service.

6. Beginning today, seek to do at least one specific act of service for your spouse each day. It is fine to do more than one. Remember your objective is to build a lifestyle of serving your spouse. Jesus said the result of your serving will be happiness (see John 13:17).

 ## SCRIPTURE MEMORY

1. Service is a way of expressing kindness. Kindness is one of the characteristics you are trying to build into your life based on the challenge in Ephesians 4:32. By now, you should be able to quote Ephesians 4:32 correctly. Always quote the reference before and after the verse. Review this verse at least once each day as you begin memorizing a second verse.

2. This week and next we will concentrate on memorizing 1 John 1:9.

> *If we confess our sins, he is faithful and just and will forgive us our sins and purify us from all unrighteousness.* (1 John 1:9)

At least three times each day this week read the reference, the verse, and the reference again. After three days of reading it, try to memorize it. Continue reviewing it daily until you are able to say it correctly.

If you feel comfortable doing so, ask your mate to help you build your list of things he would like you to do for him.

Reading,

marking,

and

discussing

with God

a chapter

from His

Word each

day should

become a

regular part

of your life.

3. For review you may want to refer to a card with the verse printed on it. Carry it with you and place it before you as you memorize. At the back of this guide you will find the verses printed in the New International Version.

▼ DAILY GROWTH EXERCISES

Conversation with God. Reading, marking, and discussing with God a chapter from His Word each day should become a regular part of your life. If you are having difficulty with this, discuss it with your group, and ask for their help. Talk with your leader. Continue to record on page 129 the chapters you are reading.

Sharing Time with My Spouse. There is no substitute for your daily sharing time with your spouse. This will keep the lines of communication open. In one of your sharing times this week, you will want to work through the learning exercise. This will open new insights into how you may better serve your spouse. Continue sharing some of the daily events of your life and your feelings about them. Record on page 131 the days you have a sharing time with your spouse.

CHAPTER ⑤

BECOMING FRIENDS
WITH MY FEELINGS

Emotions, positive and negative, are gifts from God. How dull life would be if we were not able to feel! Try to imagine watching a sunset, a ball game, or the ocean and feeling no emotion. We would be something less than human if we had no feelings. We are made in the image of God, and a part of what that means is that we are emotional creatures.

Feelings are not thoughts. Ideally we can control our thoughts, but our emotions are not nearly as manageable. Feelings are our unsolicited, inner, personal reactions to what goes on around us, or to what has happened to us in the past. Feelings are as common as breathing. Yet, many Christians talk about feelings as enemies. "My emotions are out to destroy me. I must not listen to my emotions." "Faith, not feelings, is the road to spiritual growth." These are commonly accepted statements among Christians. Why are we so critical of this aspect of our humanity? God gave us emotions for growth, maturity, fulfillment, and enjoyment. Feelings were made to be our friends.

Why do we pit ourselves against our emotions? One reason is that we have seen so many who have followed their emotions reap destruction. They have done what they *felt* like doing, and everyone around them has suffered. Another reason we don't trust feelings is that we know they change. They lift us up, and they let us down. Our highs don't last, and our lows are painful. We conclude, therefore, that emotions are unreliable and that we must

live independent of them if we are to have spiritual victory. Perhaps the chief reason we consider emotions as enemies is that negative emotions don't seem to fit in with being a "good Christian." Anger, fear, disappointment, loneliness, frustration, depression, and sorrow don't fit the stereotype of successful Christian living.

The fact is, as we shall see in our Bible study, Jesus experienced every emotion— even negative emotions. Does that mean that Jesus was not a success? Hardly! Negative and positive emotions are not good or bad. Feelings are morally neutral. It is what we do in response to our feelings that characterizes them as bad or good, sinful or righteous. In response to anger, Jesus cleared the temple of money changers and livestock —a very righteous act.

Negative and positive emotions are intended by God to be our friends. They are one of God's motivational instruments to move us in a positive direction. We may be stimulated by a positive or a negative emotion. If we are moving in the *right* direction, whatever emotion we experience is good. The emotion itself is neutral, but the results can be positive.

Many Christians tend to deny negative emotions. Said another way, many Christians are not willing to accept their feelings and then seek constructive ways of responding. Feelings are like thermometers. They report whether we are hot or cold, whether all is well, or not so well. If all is well, then we can celebrate. If emotions indicate that all is not well, we can take positive action to correct the situation. If the situation cannot be changed (example: death of a friend), we accept our emotions as indicators that we are human, and we grow through the pain. An awareness of God's presence brings comfort in the midst of our sorrow.

The Bible study and learning exercise that follow are designed to help you make friends with your feelings and learn to share some of your emotions with your spouse. Since we are emotional creatures, we cannot share life without sharing emotions.

 **BIBLE STUDY**

We will be looking at two lengthy New Testament passages, so you will need your Bible.

1. Read Mark 3:1–6. What two emotions did Jesus experience?

- ❑ Joy
- ❑ Anger
- ❑ Sorrow
- ❑ Compassion
- ❑ Love
- ❑ Depression

What external situation stimulated these emotions in Jesus? _____
_____
_____

Define *anger* in your own words. Check your answer using a dictionary. _____
_____
_____

The root word for the word *distressed* in Mark 3:5 means "pain," and is sometimes translated "sorrow or inner pain over the response of others." Write a brief description of an experience when you felt grieved. _____
_____
_____

Fear is an

emotion

that pushes

us away

from a

person,

place, or

thing.

In Mark 3:5 what action did Jesus take because of His feelings of anger and sorrow?

_____

_____

What lesson can we learn from Jesus' example? _____

_____

_____

Jesus experienced anger and sorrow in this situation in Mark 3. Let's look at other emotions Jesus experienced in the Garden of Gethsemane.

2. Read Matthew 26:36–46. What emotions did Jesus feel?

❑ Anger
❑ Sorrow
❑ Love
❑ Compassion
❑ Joy
❑ Depression

What external situations brought on these emotions? _____

_____

The word *sorrowful* in verses 37–38 is the same Greek word as *distressed* in Mark 3:5; but, the word *troubled* (NIV) is a Greek word meaning "much distressed" and is often translated "depressed." When was the last time you experienced feelings of depression? Write a brief description. _____

_____

_____

What actions did Jesus take when He felt sorrow and depression?

❑ Retreated
❑ Sought guidance from friends
❑ Prayed
❑ Involved Himself in activity

What conclusions can you draw from His example? _____
_____
_____

What emotions did Jesus feel when He said to His disciples, "Could you men not keep watch with me one hour?" (v. 40)? Check one.

- ❑ Anger
- ❑ Sorrow
- ❑ Disappointment
- ❑ Love
- ❑ Joy
- ❑ Depression

Why did He feel this way? What stimulated this emotion? _____
_____
_____

What was His response to this emotion? _____
_____

What was Jesus' prayer in verses 39 and 42? "My Father, _____
_____."

Fear is an emotion that pushes us away from a person, place, or thing. *Love* is an emotion that draws us to someone or something. *Anger* is the emotion that pits us against a person or situation. Which of these three emotions did Jesus feel when He prayed, "Father, if it is possible, may this cup pass from me" (v. 39)?

- ❑ Fear
- ❑ Love
- ❑ Anger

How did Jesus respond to this emotion? (see verses 39, 42, 46) _____

Would Jesus have been fully human if He had not felt the emotion of fear at the prospect of crucifixion and death?

❑ Yes
❑ No

Fear is a natural human emotion that normally keeps us from rushing into dangerous situations. Thus, it is one of God's blessings. Sometimes, however, God leads us into dangerous situations in which we must acknowledge our fear, trust Him, and move into the situation. Write a brief description of a situation in your life when you experienced fear. _____
_____

How did you respond in this fearful situation? _____
_____
_____

Looking back, can you think of a better way you might have responded? _____
_____
_____

Before we conclude this Bible study, let's look at one more passage that involves Jesus and His emotions.

3. Read Matthew 23:37–39. What emotions do you see reflected in Jesus' words? Check all that apply.

❑ Joy
❑ Anger
❑ Sorrow
❑ Compassion
❑ Love
❑ Depression

What brought on these emotions? _____
_____
_____

Sometimes we feel love and sorrow in much the same manner. Those we love will not always allow us to express our love, so we feel sorrow. In this situation, Jesus' love did not change the people's response. Can you think of a similar sorrow in your life? Briefly write a description. _____

_____

_____

4. From these three passages, we see that Jesus experienced positive and negative emotions. We have learned from Jesus' example how best to express our emotions. This Bible study draws our attention to the negative emotions because they tend to cause us more problems.

Negative emotions are our spontaneous response to the actions of others or to events that we find undesirable. These emotions are not sinful, but should be handled positively. Consider the following actions as you conclude this Bible study.
- Pray about the situation—share your feelings and desires with God.
- Talk with others—share your feelings in an open but kind way.
- Take positive action—ask: "What would Jesus have me do?" In His power, take the first step.

We see that Jesus experienced positive and negative emotions.

 ## LEARNING EXERCISE

Making the most of emotions involves four steps. These may be expressed in the form of four questions:
- What emotion do I feel?
- What brought on the emotion?
- Why do I feel this way?
- What will I do in response to this emotion?

Let's look closely at these four steps.

Step 1: What emotion do I feel?
The first step in becoming friends with our feelings is to identify them. Putting a label on a particular feeling is a means of identifying it. Sometimes you will have more than one emotion related to the same situation.

Emotions

usually have

a logical

explanation.

Choose an event or a situation you have encountered recently and try to identify your feelings toward it. Complete the following sentence by drawing a circle around the word or words that best describe your emotions. I feel (or felt)...

angry, fearful, disappointed, sorrowful, frustrated, discouraged, depressed, happy, excited, loved, peaceful, joyful, exhilarated, hopeful, sad, lonely, used, abused, confused, (other: _____).

Be specific in identifying your emotions.

Step 2: What brought on the emotion?
The second step in making friends with your feelings is to clarify what external stimulation triggered that emotional response. What did someone do or say, or what did you see or hear that touched an emotional nerve? _____
_____
_____

Specifically indicate the external stimulation of the emotions circled in step 1 by completing the following sentence: My feelings were brought on by _____
_____
_____

Step 3: Why do I feel this way?
The third step has to do with internal stimulation. Emotions usually have a logical explanation. If you reflect on what just happened and then take a look at yourself, you can normally understand why you feel as you do.

Identify the internal source of your emotions by answering the following question: What is there about my personality and beliefs and my past that would make me feel the way I do about this situation? _____
_____
_____

Step 4: What will I do in response to this emotion?
Once you have an understanding of how you came to feel the way you do, you are in a position to make a positive response. Perhaps you need to talk with someone about the situation, to request a change in the way certain things are done, or to ask

for clarification. Maybe sharing your feelings with a friend would help. Together you can discuss what constructive action you might take. Sometimes, no action is best. Identifying the feeling and understanding its source may be enough. Some feelings are short-lived. Reflect on the situation you identified in steps 1 through 3 and answer the following question: What positive actions should I take in response to my feelings? _____

_____

_____

_____

 ## DAILY GROWTH EXERCISES

Conversations with God. Continue to indicate on the record sheet (page 129) the chapters you read, marked, and discussed with God this week. Ask God to give you an increased desire to spend time with Him each day.

Sharing Time with My Spouse. Continue to spend 10 to 15 minutes each day sharing with your spouse some of the things that have happened during the day and how you feel about them. Record your progress on page 131.

In one of your sharing times this week, show your spouse something you have marked in your Bible recently and tell him or her why it was meaningful to you. When you have completed this, note below what you shared.

Book: _____

Chapter: _____

Verse: _____

Share with your spouse your answers to the four steps in the learning exercise.

Indicate the date you shared this: _____

SCRIPTURE MEMORY

Continue to review the two verses you have memorized. Reviewing them regularly will fix them firmly in your heart and mind. Be prepared to quote Ephesians 4:32 and 1 John 1:9 in your group this week.

LEARNING TO LISTEN

I know you believe you understand what you think I said, but I'm not sure you realize that what you heard is not what I meant.

Situations like this happen in many marriages on a daily basis. Words are said, but thoughts and feelings are not understood. Talking is only half of communication. Listening is essential if we are going to understand the words of the person speaking to us.

Since words have different meanings to different people, and since we tend to hear what we want to hear, good listening requires discipline. We must overcome the tendency to assume that we know what people mean by what they say. Active listening involves asking questions for clarification until we are certain that we understand what the other person means.

When we understand what another person means, then we can make a meaningful response. Most of us have developed a pattern of responding before we really know what the other person is saying. For example, if a husband walks in the room and says, "I'm going to quit my job," his wife might lecture him on how unwise that would be in the present economic situation, or how smart that would be considering his present situation, or how smart that would be because she never has liked that job. If she would take time to ask what he meant by what he said, she may find that he was not thinking of quitting his job, but simply was expressing that he had had a difficult day at work.

Listening is not only the road to understanding another person, it is also a means of ministering to that person. When you listen to someone, you are giving your time, your attention, your life. What a powerful way to communicate that your spouse is important to you! Listening is saying "I care. Your ideas are important to me. I want to understand how you feel." On the other hand, failing to listen or listening halfheartedly communicates the opposite. Good marriages do not exist without good listeners.

This week the Bible study will focus on principles of listening and the learning exercise will introduce you to two communication techniques to aid in active listening.

BIBLE STUDY

1. Get your Bible. Read 1 Corinthians 14:7–11. What communication problem is highlighted by Paul? Check one.

- ❑ Talking too much
- ❑ Speaking too fast
- ❑ Speaking to be understood
- ❑ Listening

Assume that you want to understand someone who speaks a different language. What are some approaches to learn what he was saying?

❑ Take a foreign language course
❑ Speak through a translator
❑ Buy a book that translates his language to yours

What element is common to all of the approaches that you noted? _____
_____
_____

2. *"For this people's heart has become calloused; they hardly hear with their ears, and they have closed their eyes"* (Acts 28:27). What does Paul say about the "ears" of his Jewish audience? Underline your answer in the verse.

What does it mean here to "hardly hear with their ears"? _____
_____
_____

What are some possible reasons the Jews did not want to hear the gospel message?

❑ Content with life as is
❑ Not willing to listen and understand
❑ Distracted by sin in their lives
❑ Indifferent to the message

Sometimes we "hardly hear" our spouse. What are some possible reasons for not hearing our spouse?

❑ Distracted
❑ Not interested in what is being discussed
❑ Daydreaming
❑ Other thoughts take priority

Give an example when you did not want to hear what your spouse was saying because you were not willing to make the necessary changes listening would require.
_____
_____

Listening is not only the road to understanding another person, it is also a means of ministering to that person.

Everyone

should be

quick to

listen, slow

to speak

and slow

to become

angry.

JAMES 1:19

Hopefully you are beginning to recognize the importance of listening, and you are willing to sharpen your listening skills. Being willing to listen is important as we shall see in the following material.

3. *"If anyone turns a deaf ear to the law, even his prayers are detestable"* (Proverbs 28:9). In your own words, what does this verse teach about listening to God? _____
_____

Is it possible for this to happen in a marriage?

❑ Yes
❑ No

What brings a person to the point of no longer being willing to listen to his or her spouse? _____
_____
_____

Has there ever been a time in your marriage when you stopped listening?

❑ Yes
❑ No

If yes, when and why? _____
_____

What can a spouse do to help a nonlistening spouse begin to listen again? _____
_____
_____

4. *"My dear brothers, take note of this: Everyone should be quick to listen, slow to speak and slow to become angry"* (James 1:19). Where is the emphasis in this verse? Check the appropriate answer:

❑ Listening
❑ Speaking

The Bible has over 1,300 references to hearing and only about 800 references to speaking. Obviously, both hearing and speaking are essential to communication, but why do you think the emphasis is given to listening? _____

_____

_____

5. *"He who answers before listening—that is his folly and his shame"* (Proverbs 18:13). What is the sign of a foolish man according to this verse? Underline your answer in the verse.

Try to remember the last time you gave an answer before you really understood what your spouse was saying. Briefly write a description of the occasion here. _____

_____

_____

What is the best way to keep this from happening again? _____

_____

_____

A part of being a good listener is asking questions for clarification. Let's consider how Jesus asked questions to clarify what He was hearing from His disciples.

6. Jesus was a master at asking questions. Read Matthew 16:13–16 in your Bible. What two questions did He ask His disciples?

1. _____

_____

2. _____

_____

What was Jesus trying to clarify by asking these questions? _____

_____

_____

Asking questions is an excellent way to clarify what someone is thinking or feeling. Think back over your day and record the last question you asked your spouse. ____

_____

_____

What were you trying to understand by asking that question? _____
_____
_____

Listening brings about rewards in the relationship. Consider the following Old
Testament passage and how it applies to your marriage.

7. Read Jeremiah 29:11–14a in your Bible. What is the promise God made to Israel?
_____
_____

What was required of Israel in order to find God? _____
_____
_____

What does it mean to seek God? _____
_____
_____

If you applied this idea to your marriage, what would it mean to seek your spouse?
_____
_____

What would be the results of such seeking? _____
_____
_____

As you look at your own efforts to deepen and strengthen your relationship with
your spouse, what improvements can you make in your seeking? (You may want to
ask your spouse for suggestions in answering this question.) _____
_____
_____

 **LEARNING EXERCISE**

Active Listening
Imagine the following conversation between a husband and wife.

Wife: "I think you need more sleep."
Husband: "Are you saying that you think I need more sleep?"
Wife: "Well, I don't know if you need more sleep or I need more sleep."
Husband: "Are you saying that you think one of us needs more sleep?"
Wife: "I don't know if it's more sleep or not. Some days I feel so cooped up in this house that I could climb the wall."
Husband: "Darling, are you saying that some days you feel like climbing the wall?"
Wife: "Well, we don't go out anymore. We used to go out for dinner once in a while."
Husband: "Are you saying that you would like to go out for dinner more often?"
Wife: "I know we can't afford to go out for dinner, but if we could go out for dessert..."
Husband: "Darling, would you like to go out for dessert?"
Wife: "Could we?"

This conversation illustrates one technique of active listening. The husband simply repeats what his wife said in the form of a question: "Are you saying...?" We exaggerated this conversation to make our point. You don't always need to use the exact words of your spouse. You may state what you think is meant by what has been said. Your question gives your spouse a chance to clarify what he or she has in mind.

Using this technique may prove humorous or annoying, depending on both your mood and the mood of your spouse. It is, however, an excellent means of getting to know what your spouse is thinking and feeling.

At least three times this week, use this technique of active listening with your spouse. Record the dates on the following lines on which these conversations took place and the subjects that you discussed.

This technique is an excellent means of getting to know what your spouse is thinking and feeling.

The techniques discussed in this exercise should become a regular part of communication with your mate.

Date: _____ Subject discussed: _____

Date: _____ Subject discussed: _____

Date: _____ Subject discussed: _____

Rating Feelings 0–10

On Monday evening a husband and wife agree that on Saturday afternoon they will go on a picnic. The week comes and goes, and on Saturday morning around 11:30 the husband is at the office. *Oh, I wish I didn't have to go on this picnic, but I know I must go because I promised.*

Meanwhile, the wife is at home thinking, *I really wish I didn't have to go on this picnic, but I know I promised and so I must go.*

The husband comes home and loads the grill in the car, while the wife prepares the hamburgers. They go on a picnic that neither of them wants!

Why did this couple not openly discuss their feelings about the picnic? Perhaps it was their deep commitment to keeping promises. Perhaps each one did not want to disappoint the other. Maybe they feared the response of their spouse if they shared their feelings. Past experience may have influenced their decision not to discuss the matter.

Rating your feelings on a scale of 0–10 is a way to discover and share with your spouse how you really feel about something without raising emotional barriers. For example, in the situation described above, what if the husband came home and said to his wife, "0 to 10—how do you feel about the picnic?" She responded, "Do you really want to know?" "Yes, I really want to know," he said. "About two," she responded. "Good, that is exactly how I feel," said the husband. Now they both understand each other's feelings and they decide not to go on the picnic.

Suppose, however, that the husband had used words instead of numbers. What if he had said, "Darling, how do you feel about this picnic?" She may have responded, "What are you trying to do, bug out on this picnic? You are always bugging out on me!" especially if he has a history of breaking promises. This response came in spite of her negative feelings about the picnic just 30 minutes earlier. Words tend to stimulate emotions. Numbers are emotionally neutral.

Notice that he said *0 to 10* before he gave the subject. When you say *0 to 10*, you call your spouse's mind to attention. You are asking for a report about feelings on a subject. Your spouse is asked to listen carefully and report accurately. Now that you have his or her attention, what is the subject? Then your spouse can focus on the subject and communicate true feelings. This technique allows you to get to the heart of how your spouse feels without the confusing emotions that words sometimes provoke.

What if one spouse says *two* and the other says *ten*? Then one has an opportunity to serve the other. With the information as to how your spouse feels, you can intelligently decide what to do.

At least twice this week, ask your spouse to report his or her feelings on a scale of 0–10. Record below the date and subject.

Date: _____ Subject discussed: _____
Date: _____ Subject discussed: _____

The two techniques discussed in this learning exercise should become a regular part of communication with your mate. Use them every time you feel they would be helpful. Your marriage will reap the benefits.

 ## SCRIPTURE MEMORY

Begin memorizing the following verse related to speaking and listening.

> *Everyone should be quick to listen, slow to speak and slow to become angry.* (James 1:19)

DAILY GROWTH EXERCISES

Conversations with God. By this time your conversations with God should be a regular part of each day. Continue to record on page 129 the passages you read, mark, and discuss with God.

Sharing Time with My Spouse. These daily sharing times with your spouse should also become a natural part of your life. Continue to share events and feelings related to daily life and other matters that either of you desire to discuss. Use the listening techniques learned this week in your sharing times. Continue to record on page 131 the days you have this sharing time with your spouse.

CHAPTER ⑦
LEARNING
TO LOVE

According to Jesus, learning to love God and learning to love your neighbor are the two greatest commandments (see Matthew 22:35–40). Yet, we often emphasize the other commandments more than love. In fact, many persons find it difficult to express what is meant by *loving God*. And certainly few things are more confusing than contemporary ideas on what it means to *love* your neighbor (and our marriage partner is our closest neighbor). This session in *A Couple's Guide to a Growing Marriage* will help you understand love and practice it.

Our society has placed a great deal of emphasis on the emotional aspects of love. This is an outgrowth of our experience-centered philosophy, which says, "What is important is how I feel." The experience of the moment is viewed as more important than commitment, fidelity, righteousness, and other biblical values. Many couples become obsessed with their feelings or lack of feelings for each other. The temporary experience of "falling in love" is unrealistically expected to last forever. When it does not, couples question the validity of their relationship. If one of them happens to have romantic feelings for someone else, the marriage is viewed as dead and a new relationship is born.

The emotional obsession that we call *falling in love* is one of the highest of all human emotions. This emotion affects all of life. Concentration on other matters is all but impossible. Our emotional energy is spent thinking about and being with the object of our love. Falling in love is the emotional dynamic that leads people to think of intimacy and dream of a happy marriage that will last forever. Almost all couples experience this emotional high in the early days of marriage. Research has shown, however, that this euphoric state has an average life span of two years. After that, the couple returns to a normal emotional state.

Movies, magazines, and popular opinion have convinced our society that this heightened emotional state—being in love—is supposed to last forever. If you lose it, the marriage is doomed. If you find it with someone else, you never will be happy without them. Thus, in search of happiness we have increased the divorce rate 700 percent in the past 100 years. Four out of five persons who divorce eventually remarry. The majority of these marriages will also end in divorce. Happiness has not been found. We operate on the false premise that in order to be happy we must be constantly in some euphoric emotional state.

Falling in love is the initial phase of a love relationship. This is what gets us started. This is the spark that ignites the engine. But there must be constant refueling if the engine is to perform over the long haul. It is this emotional refueling that keeps a marriage alive. The process of keeping your spouse's emotional tank filled must be learned. It does not come naturally; it does not just happen. Some couples never learn how to do this. When the initial euphoric state is gone, emotionally they are adrift in the sea of matrimony, without purpose or motivation.

The good news is that anyone can learn how to keep his or her spouse's love tank full. Sadly, many never try to learn because they live under the illusion that genuine love is supposed to stay alive by itself. Such thinking makes people pawns of their emotions. The truth is that love is a commitment to seek the welfare of your spouse. The methods of expressing love, however, must be learned.

The Bible study this week will focus on two areas: loving God and loving your spouse. The learning exercise will give practical love assignments.

 ## BIBLE STUDY

God's Love for Us

1. *"But God demonstrates his own love for us in this: While we were still sinners, Christ died for us"* (Romans 5:8). What does this verse tell us about the nature of God's love for us? Underline your answer in the verse.

"For God so loved the world that he gave his one and only Son, that whoever believes in him shall not perish but have eternal life" (John 3:16). What additional truth does this verse share about God's love? _____

_____

"I have loved you with an everlasting love; I have drawn you with loving-kindness" (Jeremiah 31:3). What else characterizes God's love? Circle your answer in the verse.

With three characteristics of God's love identified, let's consider what God does for those whom He loves.

2. According to Hebrews 12:5–6 what does God do for all those whom He loves? Underline your answer in the following verses. *"And you have forgotten that word of encouragement that addresses you as sons: 'My son, do not make light of the Lord's discipline, and do not lose heart when he rebukes you, because the Lord disciplines those he loves, and he punishes everyone he accepts as a son'"* (Hebrews 12:5–6).

"Our fathers disciplined us for a little while as they thought best; but God disciplines us for our good, that we may share in his holiness. No discipline seems pleasant at the time,

but painful. Later on, however, it produces a harvest of righteousness and peace for those who have been trained by it" (Hebrews 12:10–11). What is the purpose of God's discipline according to these verses? _____
_____
_____

The Greek word for God's love is *agape*, which means "having a total concern for the welfare of another." *"There is no fear in love. But perfect love drives out fear"* (1 John 4:18). When we are convinced that God loves us totally, what will be removed from our hearts according to this verse? _____
_____
_____

Our Love for God

3. *"We love [God] because he first loved us"* (1 John 4:19). According to this verse, what stimulated our love for God? _____
_____
_____

4. What is the greatest commandment of all, according to Jesus' statement in Matthew 22:36–38? Underline your answer:

> *"Teacher, which is the greatest commandment in the Law?" Jesus replied: 'Love the Lord your God with all your heart and with all your soul and with all your mind.' This is the first and greatest commandment. And the second is like it: 'Love your neighbor as yourself.' All the Law and the Prophets hang on these two commandments."*

Why do you think Jesus would elevate this commandment as number one? _____
_____
_____

5. In John 14:23–24 Jesus gave a means of measuring our love for God. *"Jesus replied, 'If anyone loves me, he will obey my teaching. My Father will love him, and we will come to him and make our home with him. He who does not love me will not obey my teaching. These words you hear are not my own; they belong to the Father who sent me.'"* In your own words, what is evidence of our love for God? _____
_____

There is no fear in love. But perfect love drives out fear.

1 JOHN 4:18

Most of us would not feel comfortable saying to a friend, "If you love me, do what I say." How can Jesus be justified in making such a statement to His followers? (In addition to John 14:23–24, see also Deuteronomy 10:12–13.) _____

_____

_____

6. *"If anyone says, 'I love God,' yet hates his brother, he is a liar. For anyone who does not love his brother, whom he has seen, cannot love God, whom he has not seen. And he has given us this command: Whoever loves God must also love his brother"* (1 John 4:20–21). According to these verses, if we truly love God, what is another way it will be evidenced? _____

_____

_____

The same Greek word that is used of God's love *(agape)* is used in the 1 John passages we have studied. Thus, to love is to have a total concern for the welfare of another. Select from your experiences this week one action that demonstrates your concern for someone else. Record that action here. _____

_____

Our Love for Our Spouses

7. Read in your Bible Ephesians 5:25–29. Two models are given for a husband's love for his wife. What are these models?

(1) _____
(2) _____

If a husband loves his wife as Christ loved the church, what will be the chief characteristic of that love? Look at verse 25. _____

_____

What are some implications of a husband's loving his wife as he loves his own body? See verses 28–29 for your answer. _____

_____

_____

Husbands, in the last 24 hours, how much time have you spent nourishing your own body? Include eating, sleeping, exercise, etc. _____

_____

_____

In the same 24 hours, how much time have you spent nourishing your wife? _____

_____

_____

List something you did during that time to nourish your wife. _____

_____

_____

The Bible also suggests that older women have a responsibility to younger women. Let's see what this says to us in the context of learning to love.

"Likewise, teach the older women to be reverent in the way they live, not to be slanderers or addicted to much wine, but to teach what is good. Then they can train the younger women to love their husbands and children" (Titus 2:3–4). According to these verses, what are the older women to do for the younger women? _____

_____

_____

In your opinion, why do younger women need the teaching and encouragement of older women to love their husbands? _____

_____

_____

"To be self-controlled and pure, to be busy at home, to be kind, and to be subject to their husbands, so that no one will malign the word of God" (Titus 2:5). In your own words note the additional things that the older women are to teach the younger women.

_____

_____

_____

Wives, which of the above do you find the most difficult to do? _____

_____

_____

Why? _____
_____
_____

8. *"Do nothing out of selfish ambition or vain conceit, but in humility consider others better than yourselves. Each of you should look not only to your own interests, but also to the interests of others. Your attitude should be the same as that of Christ Jesus"* (Philippians 2:3–5). These verses describe the attitude of love, though the word *love* is never used. Paraphrase the three descriptive statements in this passage.

_____
_____
_____

Think about last week. Note one occasion in which you regarded your spouse as more important than yourself. Write a brief, specific description. _____
_____
_____

Summarize the teaching of Philippians 2:3–5 as it applies to marriage. _____
_____
_____
_____

LEARNING EXERCISE

We recognize that in marriage love is a commitment to seek the welfare of our mates. One of our deepest emotional needs is to feel loved; that is, to feel that our mates are looking out for our interests. Most marriage partners want to meet this need, but they don't always know how. Listed below are five common ways—love languages—to express love. Read them carefully to determine which one or two are most important to you.

Words—One way to express love is simply by saying, "I love you," or "You look nice in that dress (or suit)," or, "I like the way you did that." Verbal statements affirming love bring a great deal of emotional security to some of us.

Gifts—A second love language is gifts. The gifts need not be expensive to be valuable. A gift says, "You think of me when we are apart." You cannot secure a gift

Teach the older women to be reverent in the way they live, not to be slanderers or addicted to much wine, but to teach what is good.

TITUS 2:3

When our emotional tanks are full, the whole world looks bright.

without thinking about your spouse. Giving gifts is a deliberate act of love.

Actions—Doing things for your spouse can be a powerful communication of love. Love can be expressed by such things as cooking a favorite meal, washing dishes, dusting, vacuuming the floor, taking out the garbage, or putting gas in the car.

Time—Spending quality time with your spouse is also a means of expressing love. Quality time is giving your spouse your undivided attention. Whether you are sitting on the couch, taking a walk, or sharing a meal at a quiet restaurant, when you focus attention on listening and sharing with your spouse, you are communicating love.

Touch—Physical touch is an important way to express love. Kissing, embracing, sexual intercourse, or other affectionate physical contacts are means of communicating love.

Most of us have a primary love language. One or two of the above are more important to us than the others in making us feel loved. Choose your primary love language and record it here.

My love language is _____

For most couples, the love language of one spouse is different from the other. Without talking with your spouse, what do you think is his or her primary love language? What makes your spouse feel most loved? My spouse's love language is

_____

In one of your sharing times this week, share your love languages with each other. Remember, your spouse is the expert on what makes him or her feel loved. Accept what your mate says and begin to speak that language. You will never keep your spouse's emotional tank full unless you learn to speak his or her language. By nature, we tend to speak our language, and then wonder why our spouse does not feel loved.

When our emotional tanks are full (when we really feel secure in the love of our spouses), the whole world looks bright. When our tank is empty (when we do not feel loved by our spouses), the whole world looks dark. The task of the husband is to discover the love language of his wife, and to express love so frequently that her emotional tank remains full. The wife has the same responsibility toward her husband.

Assignment: For the next two weeks we want you and your mate to play the Tank Check Game. At least three times this week, say to your spouse, "0 to 10, how's your love tank today?" Ten means that your emotional tank is running over; you can't handle any more love. Zero means your tank is completely empty and you are running on memories only. If the response is anything other than ten, ask, "What could I do to help fill it?" Whatever your mate suggests, do it to the best of your ability as an act of love. Record below the suggestions made and check when you have completed the request.

Suggestion   *Completed*

Monday _____ _____

Tuesday _____ _____

Wednesday _____ _____

Thursday _____ _____

Friday _____ _____

Saturday _____ _____

Sunday _____ _____

For a more complete understanding of the love language concept, you may want to read Gary Chapman's book *The Five Love Languages*, published by Northfield Publishing. For information on The Five Love Languages Video Pack, visit www. Lifeway.com or call (800) 458-2772.

SCRIPTURE MEMORY

Continue memorizing James 1:19. *"Everyone should be quick to listen, slow to speak and slow to become angry."* Continue reviewing Ephesians 4:32 and 1 John 1:9 several times a day. Constant review of these verses will make them a part of your daily experience. Our objective is to see our lives influenced by the truths in these verses.

DAILY GROWTH EXERCISES

Conversations with God. Continue to record on page 129 the chapters you read, mark, and discuss with God.

Sharing Time with My Spouse. You may wish to play the Tank Check Game during this sharing time. You will certainly want to discuss the love language concept shared in the learning exercise. Continue to record your sharing time on page 131.

LEARNING TO AGREE

The way a couple arrives at decisions can make or break a marriage. Communication problems in marriage often stem from disagreements in decision-making. The husband-as-dictator pattern has destroyed the creative spirit of many wives. The mother-superior attitude has made children out of many husbands. Neither of these patterns is biblical, but many Christians have accepted them as normal.

Marriage is meant to be two persons who are members on the same team. God is the coach, and the husband and wife are teammates. Successful teammates cooperate. "How can we help each other?" is the question asked by members of a winning team. God said that "It is not good for the man to be alone." Therefore, God created a "helper suitable for him" (Genesis 2:18). The word *suitable* means "one perfectly matched." The word *helper* implies that the wife is to be actively and vitally involved with her husband in the task of subduing the earth (see Genesis 1:28). This principle of cooperative endeavor applies to decision-making as well as other areas of life.

For the wife to be a helper and for the husband not to be alone in decision-making, there must be open and free communication of thoughts and feelings. Why should a husband be limited to his insights when he has a wise helper? How can a wife be a helper if she is always silent? When a husband or wife seeks to control the other, they cease to be a team. They no longer cooperate but become competitors. This was never God's intention.

Team members who cannot agree on the game plan will never be winners. Similarly, husbands and wives who cannot agree on decisions will never produce a winning marriage. The Old Testament prophet asked the question: "Do two walk together unless they have agreed to do so?" (Amos 3:3). Walking together requires coordinated effort. No less is required for harmonious marriages. Husbands and wives should always work toward agreement on decisions.

Reaching agreement, however, is a process. Individuals have personal thoughts and feelings on every subject. Our thoughts and feelings do not always agree with those of our spouses. We must listen, understand, and compromise to reach agreement. *Compromise* is not a negative word. Webster says a compromise is "a settlement by consent reached by mutual concessions." We each share our perspective and then we look for that on which we can agree. Each partner should be willing to give and to change, if each one can see the benefit to the other. The attitude of love discussed in chapter 7 is so important. Without a spirit of love—seeking the welfare of the other—we may never reach agreement.

Couples whose emotional needs are unmet have difficulty agreeing. Decision-making is often used as an arena to fight for rights. Demanding rights usually is an indication that emotional needs are unmet. The next time you are having difficulty reaching agreement, ask, "Why are we unable to get together on this matter?" "Why do we each feel so strongly about our positions?" "What does our unyielding stance tell us about ourselves emotionally?" One wife said, "I am so insecure that I fear making myself look stupid, so I resist when you ask me to join you in front of the group." Before she examined the emotional reasons for her behavior, she gave several logical arguments why standing before a group was difficult for her. Our stated reasons are most often logical; our real reasons are most often emotional. Examining these emotional reasons helps a couple gain understanding and agreement.

The Bible study this week will lead you in a discovery of the biblical pattern of decision-making. The learning exercises will help you examine your present patterns and determine if changes need to be made. The Scripture memory will focus on the attitude necessary if you are to learn to agree.

BIBLE STUDY

1. Get your Bible and read Genesis 2:18–25. How can a wife become a helper in decision-making? _____
_____
_____

What does verse 24 imply about the decisions of a married couple? _____
_____
_____

2. How would you answer this question: *"Do two walk together unless they have agreed to do so?"* (Amos 3:3). _____
_____
_____

3. In Philippians 2:2 Paul made a request of the Christians at Philippi: *"Then make my joy complete by being like-minded, having the same love, being one in spirit and purpose."* What implication does this verse have for Christian couples? _____
_____
_____

How do we reach the objective to be in agreement on decisions? Philippians 2:3–4 offers suggestions. Underline them in the following verses. *"Do nothing out of selfish*

Do not

get drunk

on wine,

which

leads to

debauchery.

Instead, be

filled with

the Spirit.

EPHESIANS 5:18

ambition or vain conceit, but in humility consider others better than yourselves. Each of you should look not only to your own interests, but also to the interests of others."

This self-giving attitude on the part of the husband and the wife is perhaps the greatest factor in obtaining unity in decisions. Who is our best example in maintaining this attitude? (See Philippians 2:5–8.) _____

4. Read Ephesians 5:18–21 in your Bible. List six instructions in these verses given to Christians.

(1) _____

(2) _____

(3) _____

(4) _____

(5) _____

(6) _____

In your own words, what does it mean to be filled with the Holy Spirit? _____
_____
_____

In what way is being filled with the Holy Spirit related to the other instructions in Ephesians 5:19–21? _____
_____
_____

We need to have the power of the Holy Spirit if we are to follow the specific instructions given to husbands and wives in Ephesians 5:22–33. List the instructions given to wives in this passage. _____
_____
_____

List the instructions given to husbands in the same passage. _____
_____
_____

Define the following words found in Ephesians 5:22, 33.

Submit (vv. 21–22): _____

_____

Respect (v. 33): _____

_____

What two examples of love are husbands given in Ephesians 5:25, 28?
1. _____
2. _____

Define the following words found in Ephesians 5:29.

Feed: _____

_____

Care for: _____

_____

Husbands, what positive changes could you make to do a better job at feeding and caring for your wife? Be specific. _____

_____

_____

Wives, what positive changes could you make to do a better job at submitting to and showing respect for your husband? _____

_____

_____

What is one of the responsibilities of the head? (See Ephesians 5:23.) What does the word *savior* mean to you? _____

_____

_____

What is the chief characteristic of love? (See Ephesians 5:25.) _____

_____

How difficult would it be for a wife to show respect and submission to a husband who, with the aid of the Holy Spirit, is caring for and giving to his wife? Place an X on the continuum:

POSSIBLE	MAYBE	IMPOSSIBLE

Which came first? Check one:

❑ The submission of the church to Christ
❑ The love of Christ for the church

Who should take the lead in following the instructions of this passage in your marriage? Check one:

❑ Husband
❑ Wife

Is the wife relieved of her responsibilities if her husband is not loving, caring, and giving? (See 1 Peter 3:1–6.)

❑ Yes
❑ No

Why? _____

What does Ephesians 5:18–33 have to do with helping a couple reach agreement in decision-making? _____
_____
_____

5. *"Now I want you to realize that the head of every man is Christ, and the head of the woman is man, and the head of Christ is God"* (1 Corinthians 11:3). The words *man* and *woman* in this verse are the same Greek words used for *husband* and *wife*. What does the phrase "the head of Christ is God" mean to you? _____
_____
_____

Using the model of God the Father as the head of God the Son, what parallels do you see between the model and the husband being the head of the wife? _____

_____

_____

6. *"Then God said, 'Let us make man in our image, in our likeness'"* (Genesis 1:26). When it comes to the matter of decisions made by God (Father, Son, and Holy Spirit), the Bible gives only limited information. What conclusion might be drawn from Genesis 1:26 regarding God's decision-making? _____

_____

_____

In Matthew 26:36–46 we read a conversation between Christ and the Father. Read it in your Bible. What two conclusions regarding decision-making can you draw from this conversation?

(1) _____

(2) _____

From Matthew 26:36–46, could you conclude that the submission of the wife means that she should never express her thoughts and feelings to her husband?

❑ Yes
❑ No

Why? _____

7. If a husband and wife openly discuss an issue and cannot reach an agreement, what should be done? _____

_____

_____

If the husband is chosen to make decisions when the spouses do not agree and the decision can wait no longer, what should be the husband's chief concern? (See Philippians 2:3–4.) _____

_____

Going a little farther, he fell with his face to the ground and prayed, "My Father, if it is possible, may this cup be taken from me."

Matthew 26:39

Husbands,

love your

wives, just

as Christ

loved the

church and

gave himself

up for her.

EPHESIANS 5:25

If the husband interprets his headship to mean that he is always to have his way, what biblical truth is he overlooking? (See Ephesians 5:25.) _____

_____

8. With this Bible study as a background, write a description of how decisions should be made in a Christian marriage. _____

_____

_____

LEARNING EXERCISE

If the goal in decision-making is agreement but the two parties do not agree after their initial discussion, what is the next step? Basically, there are three ways a couple can reach agreement and resolve the decision.

1. *"Meet you in the middle"*
In this pattern, the couple looks for a compromise somewhere in the middle between the two original positions. This middle ground will meet some of the needs of each person and will require some giving on the part of both.

For example, Mary wanted Bob to go with her to visit her parents, leaving on Friday afternoon and coming home Sunday afternoon. Bob said, "We were down there three weeks ago and I don't want to go back this soon." They have a conflict! After they listened to each other and heard the reasons and feelings, things looked different. Bob discovered that that weekend was her mother's birthday. Mary discovered there was a church softball tournament on Saturday, and she knew how important the tournament was to him. After they understood each other, they agreed to make their visit on Friday afternoon, have her mother's birthday dinner that evening, and return home on Saturday morning.

2. *"Meet you on your side"*
This pattern requires one partner to give up his or her original position and agree on the proposal of the spouse. This decision may come from the realization that one idea or plan is better or more feasible. Sometimes, however, it may be a conscious decision to put one spouse's needs above the other, recognizing the importance attached to the matter.

Using the above illustration, let's assume that there was not a softball tournament. Bob didn't want to visit Mary's parents simply because they had visited three weeks ago. He did not feel comfortable with her parents, and did not want to establish a pattern of going to see them every three weeks. After they heard each other, Bob realized that birthdays are important to Mary and agreed to meet Mary on her side. He loves Mary and knows that this is important to her, so he agreed to go with her for the weekend.

3. *"Meet you later"*
This pattern admits that for the present, agreement cannot be reached. Therefore, both parties agree to disagree temporarily. Perhaps after further prayer and discussion they can agree on one of the positions above. For now, however, they will not allow this difference to divide them. They will give each other the freedom to be different, agree to disagree, and not constantly demand that the other person change.

Let's return to our example. It was midnight. Bob and Mary shared the facts with each other, but they were not able to reach an agreement. They were both tired and sleepy. They agreed each would pray for guidance, and they would discuss it again the next evening. They assured each other of their love and affirmed that they would find an agreeable solution. They went to sleep without resentment because they agreed that they would meet later.

Sometimes, agreeing to disagree can be a permanent solution. Let's take toothpaste. She is a middle squeezer and he squeezes from the bottom (like you ought to). They ask for change but neither is able to break this lifelong habit. They agree to disagree, and buy two tubes of toothpaste. This solution will last for a lifetime or until they discover the pump!

Each of the three patterns requires understanding, loving attitudes, and willingness to change. The difference in number 3 is that each person is willing to accept the other's position, whereas before each demanded agreement.

Think about the decisions you have made the past few months. Try to find an example of each pattern. Write a brief description of what the differences were and how you resolved them.

What was your final agreement?

1. *Meet you in the middle*

We disagreed about _____

_____

We resolved it by _____

_____

2. *Meet you on your side*

We disagreed about _____

_____

We resolved it by _____

_____

Note below one decision you and your spouse have not yet agreed on. You have talked about it, but you both know that you have not yet agreed. Briefly state your position and that of your spouse.

Subject: _____

My position: _____

Position of my spouse: _____

Try to examine your emotions and answer this question: "What are my emotional reasons for holding this position?" What is it about you that makes it difficult for you to change your position? _____

_____

_____

In your sharing time this week, discuss with your spouse your answers in the learning exercise. Seek to make this a learning experience by trying to understand yourself and your spouse. A changed attitude may make agreement a much more attainable goal. In response to prayer, God often stimulates our emotions and attitudes, enabling us to break out of old patterns of thinking and feeling. If you sincerely desire agreement with your spouse, ask God to show you His perspective.

 SCRIPTURE MEMORY

This week and next we will concentrate on memorizing Philippians 2:3–4.

> *Do nothing out of selfish ambition or vain conceit, but in humility consider others better than yourselves. Each of you should look not only to your own interests, but also to the interests of others.* (Philippians 2:3–4)

This passage is longer than those you have memorized previously but its message is powerful and in it you will find many life applications. Read the reference, verses, and reference again at least three times each day this week. After three days of reading it, try to memorize it. Take it phrase by phrase. Continue reviewing it daily until you are able to say it correctly. For purpose of review you may want to write the verses on a card to carry with you or place before you for easy reference.

Continue to review your other three verses at least once each day.

 DAILY GROWTH EXERCISES

Conversations with God. Continue to record on page 129 the chapters you are reading, marking, and discussing with God each day. Be prepared to share one of these with your group each week.

Sharing time with My Spouse. This daily sharing time with your spouse is essential to building an intimate relationship. In one of your sharing times this week, discuss the learning exercise. This should help you develop a positive pattern for decision-making.

If you sincerely desire agreement with your spouse, ask God to show you His perspective.

CHAPTER 9

DEVELOPING A POSITIVE RESPONSE TO ANGER

In the last chapter, we discussed the process of learning to agree. One of the emotions that commonly hinders that process is anger. In fact, anger is the number one barrier to open, honest communication about conflicts. Anger often accompanies conflict. If a couple allows anger free rein in their marriage, they will likely destroy each other rather than find agreement. Therefore, couples must find ways to control anger as they seek agreement about whatever stimulated the anger.

As we learned in chapter 5, the emotion of anger is not a sin. Jesus felt anger, and every normal person will occasionally become angry. Sometimes our anger, like that of Jesus, comes from a concern for righteousness. We are stirred because we see an injustice or an inequity. We feel that someone else is being mistreated. At other times, our anger is the result of our misunderstanding the actions or words of another person. Once we hear their explanation, our anger subsides. Sometimes our anger is rooted in selfishness. When we don't get what we want, we get angry. Whatever the source, anger has the potential of destroying a marriage relationship if it is not controlled.

Couples typically deal with anger in one of two ways. They either explode and express their anger in violent and destructive behavior, or they hold it inside and allow it to burn and smolder. We shall see in our Bible study that neither of these ways is biblical. Both are harmful ways of dealing with anger. Both bring communication to a halt. No one wants to continue talking to a person who is uncontrollably expressing their anger. On the other hand, communication is impossible when a person is not willing to talk.

Many couples simply do not resolve conflicts because anger constantly gets in the way. They are not able to carry a conversation to its conclusion because one or both either explode or withdraw. Thus, conflicts are swept under the rug and labeled off-limits to future conversation. In time, a couple may sweep so many matters under the rug that they have nothing left to talk about. There are no safe subjects, so communication ceases, and the marriage dies.

There is an answer! Anger indicates that something in the relationship needs attention. Anger is like the alarm that calls attention to a fire. Once the firemen arrive, you can turn off the alarm and focus on putting out the fire. Similarly, when anger calls us to attention, we must turn off its alarm and focus on the problem that angered us.

Sounds logical, you say, but how do I turn off the alarm? Our Bible study and learning exercise answer that question. For many couples, this will be the most important chapter in *A Couple's Guide to a Growing Marriage.* For all couples, this chapter teaches a positive plan for responding to anger. Master this plan and anger will be your friend, leading you to genuine intimacy.

❤ BIBLE STUDY

1. *"God is a righteous judge, a God who expresses his wrath every day"* (Psalm 7:11). What does Psalm 7:11 tell us about God? Underline your answer in the verse.

2. Read Mark 3:1–5 in your Bible. What provoked Christ to anger? Pay special attention to verse 5. _____ _____ _____

3. Read Jonah 3:10–4:11. What did God do that provoked anger in Jonah's heart? _____ _____

Why did this make Jonah angry? (See vv. 2–3.) _____ _____ _____

What further events compounded Jonah's anger? (See vv. 5–8.) _____ _____ _____

How did God deal with Jonah's anger? (See vv. 9–11.) _____ _____ _____

4. Read the account of the two sons in Luke 15:11–32. In your own words, explain why the older brother became angry. _____ _____

What steps did the father take to respond to the anger of his son? _____ _____ _____

5. In neither of the cases of Jonah and the older brother are we told the outcome of the anger. We are only told what God and the father did in response to the anger.

When anger calls us to attention, we must turn off its alarm and focus on the problem that angered us.

What conclusion can be drawn from these illustrations regarding our responsibility toward an angry person? _____

_____

6. *"In your anger do not sin': Do not let the sun go down while you are still angry, and do not give the devil a foothold"* (Ephesians 4:26–27). What three conclusions regarding anger can be drawn from these verses?

(1) _____

(2) _____

(3) _____

When we allow anger to remain in our hearts, what are we doing? (See v. 27.) _____

_____

7. *"My dear brothers, take note of this: Everyone should be quick to listen, slow to speak and slow to become angry, for man's anger does not bring about the righteous life that God desires"* (James 1:19–20). What are the three challenges found in verse 19?

(1) _____

(2) _____

(3) _____

How are the first two challenges related to the last one? _____

_____

In your own words, what does verse 20 mean? _____

_____

8. Read the following verses and write a paraphrase of each verse. You might want to read each verse in two translations.

Proverbs 14:17 _____

_____

Proverbs 14:29 _____

_____

Proverbs 19:11 _____

_____

Proverbs 29:11 _____

_____

Do not let the sun go down while you are still angry, and do not give the devil a foothold.

Ephesians 4:26–27

Proverbs 29:20 _____

_____

Proverbs 29:22 _____

_____

According to these verses, what is our responsibility when we get angry? _____

_____

9. There is a difference between controlling anger and suppressing anger. Clarify the difference by completing the following sentences.

(1) Controlling anger is _____

(2) Suppressing anger is _____

Suppressing anger is never encouraged in the Bible. *"But now you must rid yourselves of all such things as these: anger, rage, malice, slander, and filthy language from your lips"* (Colossians 3:8). What does this verse suggest we are to do with anger? _____

_____

_____

10. Read Ephesians 4:26 again. How long should we allow anger to remain in our hearts? _____

_____

11. You have memorized Ephesians 4:32, which challenges us to be kind, compassionate, and forgiving. According to Ephesians 4:31, what sometimes hinders us from obeying this challenge? *"Get rid of all bitterness, rage and anger, brawling and slander, along with every form of malice."* _____

_____

What practical suggestions can you give on how to *get rid of* or *rid yourselves* of anger from your heart as we are challenged in Ephesians 4:31 and Colossians 3:8?

_____

_____

 **LEARNING EXERCISE**

In this exercise we will identify two negative, destructive responses to anger and one positive, constructive response.

Negative, Destructive Responses to Anger

1. *Blowing Up*—The ventilation of anger is aimed at hurting the other person. This anger may be expressed in physical or verbal abuse. Both are destructive. In the Bible study, we were taught that a person who gives full vent to his anger is considered a fool (see Proverbs 29:11). Unfortunately, most of us have ventilated our anger occasionally and thus acted foolishly. Note the last time you remember taking out your anger on your spouse in this manner. Describe briefly the experience. _____

_____

_____

What does 1 John 1:9 instruct us to do when we have sinned in this manner? Underline your answer: *"If we confess our sins, he is faithful and just and will forgive us our sins and purify us from all unrighteousness"* (1 John 1:9).

Have you confessed this sin and asked forgiveness of your spouse?

❑ Yes
❑ No

2. *Clamming Up*—The opposite of ventilation is internalizing anger: holding it inside, refusing to talk about it, silently suffering. We were taught in the Bible study that such response is also sinful (see Ephesians 4:27, 31; Colossians 3:8). Clamming up not only violates Scripture, but it also injures the body, making us irritable, tense, and miserable. Briefly describe the last time in your marriage you responded to anger by clamming up. _____

_____

_____

Have you confessed this sin and asked forgiveness of your spouse?

❑ Yes
❑ No

Positive, Constructive Responses to Anger

Consider the following four steps to help you respond positively to anger.

- *Admit that you are angry.* Remember, the feeling of anger is not sin. Even Jesus felt anger. We should not be threatened by admitting that we feel angry. Saying, "I feel angry right now," is the first step toward resolving the problem that brought on the anger.
- *Restrain your response.* "*A fool gives full vent to his anger, but a wise man keeps himself under control*" (Proverbs 29:11). This does not mean that we should clam up. Rather it means we are to refuse to let anger drive us to an uncontrollable response. We must refuse to attack the other person verbally or physically.
- *Share your problem.* Something has happened to stimulate anger inside you. You have a problem; you are heated up about a situation you feel needs action. A temporary time-out to allow the temperature to drop is advisable, but withdrawing and refusing to share the problem with your spouse is not a good answer. You are on the same team. Share your problems, and together look for a solution.
- *Look for a solution.* A husband and wife admitting anger, restraining responses, sharing problems, and looking for solutions will find them. Listening to each other's problems with a desire to understand and love will lead to agreeable solutions. Solutions often involve changes in behavior or communication patterns. Sometimes the attitude of the one who is angry changes after he or she hears an explanation of the spouse's motives. Solutions forged out of honest, loving conversations build intimacy in a marriage.

The following statements will help you apply these steps to life:

- "I'm feeling angry right now."
- "But don't worry, I will not attack you."
- "When you have time, I would like your help in solving a problem."

When you sit down to talk begin by saying:

- "My problem is this: I feel angry when…I really need your help in finding a solution."

Read the above statements until you can say them without referring to them. Say them aloud to yourself until you feel comfortable with them. Sign off when you

Listening to each other's problems with a desire to understand and love will lead to agreeable solutions.

Sharing

each day

will allow

you to deal

with anger

as it arises

and not

let it get

bottled up.

complete this assignment: _____

After you feel comfortable saying these statements aloud, repeat them to your spouse when you are not angry. This is simply to practice the process, so that when you do get angry, you will follow the plan. Do this on three different days, when you are not angry. Sign off each day you complete this assignment:

I shared anger statements with my spouse _____
I shared anger statements with my spouse _____
I shared anger statements with my spouse _____

The next time you feel anger, follow the plan and find a solution to your problem. Record the results below.

(1) What was the problem that stimulated anger? _____
_____

(2) How closely did you follow the plan? _____
_____

(3) What solution was reached? _____
_____
_____

(4) If a solution was not found, what hindered you and your spouse from finding a solution? _____

SCRIPTURE MEMORY

Continue to memorize and review Philippians 2:3–4. Applying this verse to your marriage will help you find solutions as you discuss problems with your spouse.

Continue to review at least once each day the other three verses you have memorized. Next group session you will be asked to quote all three of them.

DAILY GROWTH EXERCISES

Conversations with God. Continue to record on page 129 the chapters you are reading, marking, and discussing with God each day. Be prepared to share one of these with your group each week.

Sharing Time with My Spouse. This brief sharing time each day will help you keep in touch with each other emotionally. This week you will use part of your sharing time to complete the learning exercise on handling anger constructively. Sharing each day will allow you to deal with anger and frustration as they arise and not let them get bottled up inside of you and your spouse.

LEARNING THE MINISTRY OF INTERCESSION

ore things have been wrought by prayer than this world dreams of."[1] In your daily quiet time, you have been conversing with God. That is the essence of prayer. Prayer is sharing your thoughts with God. Prayer may take the form of:

Adoration—praising God for who He is

Confession—agreeing with God about our sin

Thanksgiving—gratitude for God's goodness

Supplication—asking God

When we consider the ACTS acrostic, *intercession* (the ministry of praying for other) falls into the category of supplication. Intercession is *interceding* on behalf of others, asking God to respond to their needs. Unfortunately, we normally think of supplication as requesting things for ourselves. Both personal requests and intercession for others are encouraged in Scripture. Intercession for others is a ministry, while supplication for personal needs is a privilege. This chapter will focus on the ministry of intercession.

Martin Luther said, "As it is the business of tailors to make clothes and cobblers to mend shoes, so it is the business of Christians to pray."[2] Intercession is one ministry that requires no spiritual gift. All Christians are equipped for this ministry.

Not only is intercessory prayer a ministry, it is also a responsibility. Samuel said, "Far be it from me that I should sin against the LORD by failing to pray for you" (1 Samuel 12:23). Every Christian has the responsibility to intercede for others. Prayer is foundational because without it,

whatever else we claim to do in ministry will be ineffective. The teaching, preaching, or missionary ministry of the church will not be productive apart from prayer. E. M. Bounds analyzed the situation correctly when he wrote, "Talking to men is a great thing, but talking to God for men is greater still. He will never talk well and with real success to men for God who has not learned well how to talk to God for men. More than this, prayerless words in the pulpit and out of it are deadening words."[3]

Intercessory prayer is an absolute necessity for two reasons. The first reason is that God has ordained such prayer as a means of accomplishing His will in the world. James says: "You do not have, because you do not ask God" (James 4:2b). The second reason prayer is necessary is that God has commanded His people to pray. In our Bible study, we will look at Scriptures that record these commands. The command to pray must be taken as seriously as the commands to teach and preach.

The Scriptures reveal guidelines for intercessory prayer. We will examine these in the Bible study. We will also begin memorizing Jeremiah 33:3, one of the great prayer promises of the Bible. In our learning exercise we will discuss and practice conversational intercessory prayer. This form of prayer will strengthen your marriage as you and your spouse pray together. Perhaps nothing offers more potential for expanding your ministry than intercessory prayer. Let's begin our Bible study with the petition that the disciples brought to Jesus, "Lord, teach us to pray" (Luke 11:1).

 **BIBLE STUDY**

Biblical Examples of Intercessory Prayer
All of the great leaders in the Bible knew the power of intercessory prayer.

Abraham pleaded with God to spare Sodom and Gomorrah for the sake of 50, 45, 40, 30, 20, or 10 righteous people living in the city. God agreed, but 10 righteous people were not found, so God delivered Abraham's nephew Lot and his two daughters. (See Genesis 18:16–19:29.)

Moses interceded for Israel after they had built the golden calf to worship. God in His holy anger was ready to destroy them, but Moses pleaded for mercy and God responded. (See Exodus 32:7–14, 30–35.)

Joshua prayed after the defeat at Ai and God revealed the reason for the defeat—sin. Joshua responded by punishing the offender and God's blessing returned to Israel. (See Joshua 7:1–26.)

Daniel fasted and prayed in great humility, confessing his sins and the sins of Israel, seeking God's mercy after the Babylonian captivity. (See Daniel 9:1–19.)

Paul prayed for the Christians at Colosse that they would be filled with the knowledge of God's will, spiritual wisdom, and understanding. He prayed that they would live a life worthy of the Lord: bearing fruit, growing in the knowledge of God, strengthened by God's power so they could endure with patience and joy. (See Colossians 1:9–14.)

Jesus prayed for Peter that his faith would not fail under testing. (See Luke 22:31–32.)

Biblical Guidelines for Intercessory Prayer
Read the following passages and state in your own words the guideline or principle for effective intercessory prayer.
Matthew 7:7–8: _____

_____

John 16:23–24: _____

_____

James 4:2b–3: _____

_____

1 John 5:14–15; Matthew 26:39: _____

_____

Psalm 66:18; Isaiah 59:1–2: _____

_____

Hebrews 11:6: _____

_____

John 15:7: _____

_____

1 John 3:21–24: _____

_____

If you

remain in

me and

my words

remain in

you, ask

whatever

you wish,

and it

will be

given you.

JOHN 15:7

Prayer and the Marriage Relationship
"Husbands, in the same way be considerate as you live with your wives, and treat them with respect as the weaker partner and as heirs with you of the gracious gift of life, so that nothing will hinder your prayers" (1 Peter 3:7).

According to this verse, how may a husband's prayers be hindered? _____

_____

_____

List the two reasons Peter gives that a husband should honor his wife.

(1) _____
(2) _____

In what way is the wife to be considered the "weaker vessel"? _____

_____

_____

What is meant by the wife being "heirs with you of the gracious gift of life"? _____

_____

_____

Peter gives several practical principles that can be applied to husband-wife relationships. Circle or underline the specific instructions given in each verse of 1 Peter 3:8–11:

8 Finally, all of you, live in harmony with one another; be sympathetic, love as brothers, be compassionate and humble.
9 Do not repay evil with evil or insult with insult, but with blessing, because to this you were called so that you may inherit a blessing.
10 For, Whoever would love life and see good days must keep his tongue from evil and his lips from deceitful speech.
11 He must turn from evil and do good; he must seek peace and pursue it.

For the eyes of the Lord are on the righteous and his ears are attentive to their prayer, but the face of the Lord is against those who do evil (1 Peter 3:12). According to this verse, how is our treatment of each other related to answered prayer? _____

_____

Prayer Quotient Inventory
Listed below are the 10 principles in 1 Peter 3:8–11. Check to see if you discovered all of them. We have paraphrased each one and put them in the form of "I" statements in order for you to rate yourself. First, read the statement. Then, in the column to the right, evaluate yourself on a 0–10 scale. Ten means you really excel in this trait, and zero means you do very poorly.

SCORE

1. I genuinely seek to find harmony with my spouse by asking questions, listening, and sharing my thoughts and feelings until we reach agreement. _____

2. I am sympathetic and understanding when my spouse is trying to share something with me. _____

3. I regularly seek to say and do things that I feel will encourage my mate. _____

4. I normally put the interests of my spouse above my own interests. _____

5. I treat my spouse kindly and courteously in private and in public. _____

6. I do not return "evil for evil" or "insult for insult" when my spouse does or says something hurtful to me. _____

7. When my spouse has hurt or wronged me, I try to say or do
    something positive for my mate.   _____

8. I control my speech so that I will not say things that are
    deceitful or damaging to my spouse.   _____

9. I consciously say no to the evil thoughts that sometimes
    cross my mind, and seek to do something good instead.   _____

10. I am pursuing "peace" or "intimate oneness" with my mate
    as one of my major goals in life.   _____

TOTAL SCORE

_____

Your total score will give you not your IQ (intelligence quotient) but your PQ
(prayer quotient). In one of your sharing times discuss this inventory with your
spouse. Decide on one area you will seek to improve. Record below the date on
which you complete this discussion, and the area you chose to improve.

Date discussed: _____

I will seek to improve number _____

🖋 LEARNING EXERCISE

Many couples find it difficult to pray together. There are many reasons why these
couples feel uncomfortable with prayer. One reason we have just discovered in
our Bible study is that the marriage partners are not treating each other with love
and respect. Therefore, they are not motivated to pray together. The answer to this
problem is confession (see 1 John 1:9) and repentance. Other marriage partners
never learned to pray with someone else, and therefore never established the practice
of praying with their spouse. You may pray regularly with your spouse, or you may
never have prayed together, but this learning exercise will guide you and give you
experience.

Prayer takes many forms, but we will be encouraging what is called *conversational
prayer.* In conversational prayer, the husband and wife take turns talking to God
about a specific matter. They may each speak one or more times about the same
subject. When neither has further thoughts, one of them changes the subject and

they repeat the process, much as they would in a conversation with friends. Here is an example of a conversational prayer.

Husband: "Father, I want to thank You for protecting me on the way home from work today. I know that I could easily have had an accident when the truck ran the red light in front of me. I am grateful for Your protection."

Wife: "Father, I, too, thank You for protecting Don. I know that there are many accidents each day and sometimes I take Your protection for granted. Along with protection, I want to thank You for health. As I think about our good health, I also think about Don's father and his illness. I pray that You would renew his health."

Husband: "Father, I, too, pray for Dad. I pray that You would guide the doctors in this series of tests. Give them wisdom in discerning the problem and how to correct it. I pray also that You would give Dad peace of mind during this time of uncertainty."

Wife: "I also ask that You would comfort Don's mother. Remind her that You are with her and Dad through this experience."

Husband: "Also, Father, I pray that You would give her physical strength to visit Dad. You know how important she is to him." *(After a brief pause, either husband or wife may change the subject and begin praying about something else.)*

This couple may pray as long as they like and cover as many subjects as they like. When one is ready to cease praying he or she may do so by saying, "Father, thank You for this prayer time together." The other may make further comments to God and then say *Amen* or may simply say *Amen* without further comments.

Where you pray is a matter of choice. Some couples like to have a time of conversational prayer immediately after a meal while seated at the table. Others prefer the comfort of the couch or their favorite chair. Still others prefer praying before going to bed. Find the time and place that you like best.

For the purpose of this learning exercise we ask you and your spouse to have a conversational prayer time at least three days this week. Record on the next page the date and approximate time of day you shared in conversational prayer with your spouse.

In conversational prayer, the husband and wife take turns talking to God about a specific matter.

Call to me

and I will

answer you

and tell you

great and

unsearchable

things you

do not know.

JEREMIAH 33:3

Date: _____ Time of Day: _____

Date: _____ Time of Day: _____

Date: _____ Time of Day: _____

SCRIPTURE MEMORY

1. Begin memorizing Jeremiah 33:3, one of the great prayer promises of the Bible. *"Call to me and I will answer you and tell you great and unsearchable things you do not know"* (Jeremiah 33:3).

2. Continue to review Philippians 2:3–4. As you can see, the application of this verse in your marriage is also related to answered prayer.

3. Write from memory the three other verses that you have memorized.
Ephesians 4:32: _____

_____

1 John 1:9: _____

_____

James 1:19: _____

_____

DAILY GROWTH EXERCISES

Conversations with God. Continue to record on page 129 the chapters you are reading, marking, and discussing with God each day. Be prepared to share one of these with your group next week.

Sharing Time with My Spouse. Continue to record on page 131 the days you have a sharing time. Hopefully, you are developing consistency in this practice. In one of your sharing times, discuss with your spouse the Prayer Quotient Inventory, which you completed on pages 99 to 100.

NOTES

[1] Harold Lindsell, *When You Pray* (Grand Rapids: Baker, 1969), 181.

[2] W. H. A. Pritchard, *Real Prayer Explained* (London: n.d.), 9.

[3] E. M. Bounds, *Power Through Prayer* (Chicago: Moody, n.d.), 27.

CHAPTER 11

MAKING MONEY AN ASSET TO MARRIAGE

Most couples believe that if they had another hundred dollars a month, they could make it! Regardless of their present income, they need just a little more to balance the budget. The fact is, most money problems in marriage would not be solved by larger incomes. Usually problems lie not in the amount of income, but in attitudes toward money and the way money is handled. A national survey indicated that 64 percent of American couples frequently quarrel over each other's spending habits and their mutual inability to keep track of money outflow.

We come to marriage with our own ideas about how money is to be spent, how much we should save, how much we should give, and other matters related to money management. We often have strong emotional attachments to our attitudes toward money. When we find our ideas conflict with those of our spouse, our emotional stability is threatened. A wife who finds security in having substantial savings for a rainy day will be frustrated with a husband who habitually spends everything he makes. A husband who is a conservative spender will feel anger toward a wife who insists on buying new clothes each week. A person who regularly gave 10 percent to the Lord before marriage will experience inner conflict if his or her spouse is not willing to tithe.

There is no quick solution to getting together financially in a marriage, but each couple can and must find a way to do it.

The process requires talking, listening, understanding, and seeking a new way—not my way or your way, but *our* way. We must try to understand why we feel and think as we do, and we must be willing to change. If we dogmatically refuse to understand the viewpoint of our mate and reject change, finances can destroy the marriage. Of what value is money if we cannot agree on how to handle it?

Jesus said, "A man's life does not consist in the abundance of his possessions" (Luke 12:15). Life's meaning is found, not in money, but in intimate relationships. Marriage is meant to be the most intimate of all human relationships. We must not allow our conflicts over money to destroy our intimacy. We are called to unity and oneness. Reaching agreement must be a high priority.

The Bible study that follows will help you examine your ideas about money in the light of Scripture. You will find that the Bible is explicit about money. God's Word clearly affirms the lordship of Christ over our finances. God has given us guidance toward real financial freedom. We are wise if we discover and practice these sound financial principles.

The learning exercise will help you take initial steps in examining your attitudes and emotions related to money and how they differ from those of your spouse. You also will be challenged to negotiate constructive changes that will make you a better money-management team.

BIBLE STUDY

First Financial Responsibility
1. *"Honor the LORD with your wealth, with the firstfruits of all your crops; then your barns will be filled to overflowing"* (Proverbs 3:9–10).

According to these verses, what is the Christian's first financial responsibility?

_____

_____

What promise does God give to those who meet this responsibility? _____

_____

_____

2. What was the pattern of giving that God required of Israel? (See Leviticus 27:30–33.) _____

_____

3. Read in your Bible Malachi 3:8–12. How did God look upon Israel's failure to tithe? _____

_____

_____

What commitment did God make to His people if they would be faithful in tithing?

_____

_____

4. *"Woe to you, teachers of the law and Pharisees, you hypocrites! You give a tenth of your spices—mint, dill and cumin. But you have neglected the more important matters of the law—justice, mercy and faithfulness. You should have practiced the latter, without neglecting the former"* (Matthew 23:23). What was Jesus' attitude toward tithing? Underline key phrases in this verse that indicate what His attitude was.

5. Many Christians have given testimony to the truth of Proverbs 11:24–25. Read these verses and state the truth in your own words. *"One man gives freely, yet gains even more; another withholds unduly, but comes to poverty. A generous man will prosper; he who refreshes others will himself be refreshed"* (Proverbs 11:24–25). _____

_____

God's Word

clearly

affirms the

lordship of

Christ over

our finances.

A prudent

man sees

danger and

takes refuge,

but the

simple keep

going and

suffer for it.

Proverbs 22:3

Second Financial Responsibility

6. The Christian has a second area of financial responsibility. According to 1 Timothy 5:8, what is this responsibility and how important is it? *"If anyone does not provide for his relatives, and especially for his immediate family, he has denied the faith and is worse than an unbeliever."*

Responsibility: _____

Importance:
❑ Very important
❑ Somewhat important
❑ Not important

7. *"For even when we were with you, we gave you this rule: 'If a man will not work, he shall not eat.' We hear that some among you are idle. They are not busy; they are busybodies. Such people we command and urge in the Lord Jesus Christ to settle down and earn the bread they eat"* (2 Thessalonians 3:10–12). What is the Christian's challenge in these verses? _____

_____

_____

8. In your Bible, read Proverbs 24:30–34. According to this passage, what happens to the man who refuses to work? _____

_____

_____

9. How is giving to God related to providing for our families' needs? (See Matthew 6:31–33.) _____

_____

_____

What are some of the things that keep people from having enough money to meet family needs? Circle your answer in Proverbs 21:17: *"He who loves pleasure will become poor; whoever loves wine and oil will never be rich."* _____

_____

_____

Third Financial Responsibility

10. Circle in the following verse a third area of financial responsibility. *"In the house of the wise are stores of choice food and oil, but a foolish man devours all he has"* (Proverbs 21:20).

According to this verse, what is the sign of a foolish man? _____
_____
_____

11. *"A prudent man sees danger and takes refuge, but the simple keep going and suffer for it"* (Proverbs 22:3). What implications does this verse have for financial management? _____
_____
_____

12. Time to use your Bible again. How does the parable of Jesus recorded in Matthew 25:14–30 relate to the concept of saving money? _____
_____
_____

13. What guidelines do the following verses give about making sound investments? *"A simple man believes anything, but a prudent man gives thought to his steps"* (Proverbs 14:15). *"Plans fail for lack of counsel, but with many advisers they succeed"* (Proverbs 15:22). _____
_____
_____

14. Read the following Proverbs and briefly summarize the truth of each one in your own words. You might want to read each one in more than one translation.

Proverbs 11:28 _____
Proverbs 16:8 _____
Proverbs 22:7 _____
Proverbs 28:20 _____
Proverbs 30:8–9 _____

15. *"For the love of money is a root of all kinds of evil. Some people, eager for money, have wandered from the faith and pierced themselves with many griefs"* (1 Timothy 6:10). What is the warning found in this verse? Circle your answer in the verse.

16. Make a list of some of the "evils" people get caught up in while pursuing money.

(1) _____

(2) _____

(3) _____

(4) _____

(5) _____

(6) _____

17. What is the challenge of Matthew 6:24, 33? *"No one can serve two masters. Either he will hate the one and love the other, or he will be devoted to the one and despise the other. You cannot serve both God and Money....But seek first his kingdom and his righteousness, and all these things will be given to you as well."* _____

_____

_____

LEARNING EXERCISE

We can do three things with money: save it, spend it, or give it away! The following questions will help you identify your attitudes and feelings in these three areas.

Money is for saving. "Don't let it get away!" What percentage of your income would you like to save? _____ percent.

What do you plan to do with the money you save? _____

_____

_____

What life experiences have contributed to developing your present attitudes toward saving money? _____

_____

_____

What does saving money do for you emotionally? _____
_____
_____

Money is for spending. "You can't take it with you!" What percentage of your income would you like to spend? _____ percent.

List some of the things for which you spend money. _____
_____
_____

What does spending money for these things do for you emotionally? _____
_____
_____

What in your past experience has contributed to your attitude about spending money? _____
_____

Money is for giving. "God loves a cheerful giver!" What percentage of your income would you like to give away? _____ percent.

To what organizations or persons do you wish to give money? _____
_____

What has influenced your attitude about giving? _____
_____

What does giving money do for you emotionally? _____
_____

It is common for a husband and wife to have different attitudes toward saving, spending, and giving money. These attitudes are also tied to emotional needs. That is why we often feel threatened emotionally when our spouses handle money differently. We must first of all try to understand ourselves and why we respond the way we do. Also, we must seek to understand our mates and why they think

It is common for a husband and wife to have different attitudes toward saving, spending, and giving money. These attitudes are also tied to emotional needs.

and feel as they do. Then we must seek to find a new way to handle finances that will take into account our emotional needs, and yet be something on which we can both agree. We cannot remain rigidly bound to our former system without regard to our spouse's feelings. We must listen, understand, and find our way of handling finances. Unless we take the time and effort to do this, money can become a divisive factor in our marriage.

In one of your sharing times this week, discuss your answers with your spouse with a view of understanding each other better. If you identify areas of conflict, seek to find a new way of doing things. Try this new way for a month. You may have to make additional changes before you find a completely satisfactory method for both of you. Note below the date you have this sharing time.

Date completed: _____

SCRIPTURE MEMORY

1. This chapter, we will begin memorizing Luke 12:15. *"Then he said to them, 'Watch out! Be on your guard against all kinds of greed; a man's life does not consist in the abundance of his possessions'"* (Luke 12:15).

In this verse Jesus is talking to His disciples, reminding them that life's meaning is not found in material possessions. Our relationships with God and each other are far more important than all the money we will earn in a lifetime. For the purpose of review you may want to write this verse on a card, which you can carry with you or place before you.

2. Continue to review the five other verses at least once a day. Be prepared to quote these to your group this week.

DAILY GROWTH EXERCISES

Conversations with God. Continue to record on page 129 the chapters you are reading, marking, and discussing with God each day. Hopefully your time with God is becoming a vital part of your day, and you will want to continue this practice after you have completed *A Couple's Guide to a Growing Marriage.*

Be on your guard against all kinds of greed; a man's life does not consist in the abundance of his possessions.

Luke 12:15

Sharing Time with My Spouse. In one of your sharing times this week, you will want to share your learning exercise and record on page 131 when you complete it. This daily sharing time with your spouse is essential to a growing relationship. Plan to continue it as a regular part of your marriage.

DEVELOPING MUTUAL SEXUAL FULFILLMENT

Mutual sexual fulfillment has become an elusive dream for many married couples. Sexual intercourse, designed by God to be a deep expression of unity, has instead become a source of conflict and disunity. Many wives feel exploited, and many husbands rejected. The sexual joy that they once thought would come naturally in their marriage now seems impossible.

Sexual oneness, where both the husband and wife have a genuine sense of sexual fulfillment, does not come automatically. Sexual oneness is the result of asking, listening, and learning. Most young married couples genuinely desire to bring pleasure to each other sexually, but many fail to understand that the process must be learned.

In 1 Corinthians 7, husbands and wives are challenged to meet each other's sexual needs. They are warned not to cheat each other in this area of marriage. A Christian couple must take seriously the responsibility for mutual sexual fulfillment. We must learn the basic differences between male and female sexual needs and responses. We must also learn the unique feelings and desires of our spouses. This cannot happen without open communication. Doing what comes naturally will never lead us to sexual oneness.

The purpose of this chapter in *A Couple's Guide to a Growing Marriage* is to help you develop a greater openness in communication with your spouse about sexual matters. The Bible study will provide a positive perspective of Scripture regarding sexual intercourse within marriage. It will give you a clearer understanding of what God intended when He made us sexual creatures and instituted marriage. You will see that sexual intercourse is meant to be far more than the means of physical reproduction.

The learning exercise will help you discover the individual likes and dislikes of your spouse in matters related to sexual intercourse. It will be extremely important that you listen carefully to each other and be open to change. Remember, your objective is to learn to please your spouse. If both of you can reach this objective, you will find mutual sexual fulfillment. Many of you will also want to do the optional assignment that involves obtaining one or more of the suggested books. Working through these books will help answer questions you may have. A close reading, followed by open discussion, and a willingness to change will lead you to a new level of sexual fulfillment.

 **BIBLE STUDY**

1. Let's start at the beginning—Genesis. Get your Bible and locate Genesis 1:26–27, 31. What conclusions regarding the origin and nature of sex can be drawn from these verses? _____

_____

_____

2. Since God made us male and female, we would expect Him to give us guidelines for relating to each other sexually. What boundaries for sexual intercourse are found in the following verses? Underline your answers.

"You shall not commit adultery" (Exodus 20:14).
"Marriage should be honored by all, and the marriage bed kept pure, for God will judge the adulterer and all the sexually immoral" (Hebrews 13:4).

3. Read 1 Corinthians 6:15–20 in your Bible. What reasons are given for God's prohibition of adultery and sexual immorality? _____

_____

_____

4. Read 1 Corinthians 7:1–5 in your Bible. According to verses 3-4, what are the sexual responsibilities of husbands and wives? _____

_____

_____

In verse 5, Paul says that if we are not meeting each other's sexual needs, we are depriving each other. What is the one exception to regular sexual intercourse that Paul allows in this verse? _____

_____

_____

What warning does Paul give about abstaining from intercourse for the purpose of prayer? _____

_____

Sexual intercourse, designed by God to be a deep expression of unity, has instead become a source of conflict and disunity.

The term

one flesh

speaks of

intimacy or

companion-

ship; it is the

opposite of

loneliness.

5. Let's go back to Genesis. What is one of the obvious purposes of sexual intercourse within marriage according to this verse? Circle your answer: *"God blessed them and said to them, 'Be fruitful and increase in number; fill the earth and subdue it. Rule over the fish of the sea and the birds of the air and over every living creature that moves on the ground'"* (Genesis 1:28).

Circle an additional purpose for sexual intercourse stated in Genesis 2:18, 24: *"The LORD God said, 'It is not good for the man to be alone. I will make a helper suitable for him.'...For this reason a man will leave his father and mother and be united to his wife, and they will become one flesh."*

The term *one flesh* speaks of intimacy or companionship; it is the opposite of loneliness. What do you feel is necessary in a marriage for the sexual experience to be a genuine expression of companionship? _____
_____
_____

6. The sexual relationship is also intended for pleasure. *"If a man has recently married, he must not be sent to war or have any other duty laid on him. For one year he is to be free to stay at home and bring happiness to the wife he has married"* (Deuteronomy 24:5). The word *happiness* in Deuteronomy 24:5 means "to know sexually and understand what is exquisitely pleasing to her" in the physical relationship. What were God's instructions for newly married couples in Israel, according to this verse? _____
_____
_____

What does this verse tell us about sexual adjustment in marriage? _____
_____
_____

7. First Corinthians 2:11 indicates that you alone are the expert on your inner thoughts and feelings. *"For who among men knows the thoughts of a man except the man's spirit within him? In the same way no one knows the thoughts of God except the Spirit of God."* What implications does this truth have for a couple's sexual adjustment? _____
_____
_____

8. Do you find it easy or difficult to talk with your spouse about your sexual desires?

❑ Easy
❑ Difficult

Why? _____
_____
_____

Where do you feel the need for growth in your sexual adjustment with your spouse? (This is a personal question, not to be discussed with your study group.) _____
_____
_____

 LEARNING EXERCISE

Open communication is a necessity if you are to obtain the degree of satisfaction God desires in your sexual relationship. The following learning exercise is taken from Gary Chapman's book *The Marriage You've Always Wanted.* The suggestions listed in this exercise have come from husbands and wives who have attended Gary Chapman's Marriage Seminar. They are printed on the following pages in their original form, retaining the language of the individuals who submitted them. Please use your own interpretation of the terms used.

Suggestions Wives Have Made to Husbands
    How to Make Sexual Relations More Meaningful
Wives, read the following list and check those items you would like to mention to your husband.

❑ 1. Show more affection, attention throughout the day; come in after work and kiss my neck.
❑ 2. Spend more time in foreplay; love, play, and romantic remarks are important.
❑ 3. Encourage sex act at various times rather than always at night when tired.
❑ 4. Be more sympathetic when I am really sick.
❑ 5. Be the aggressive one instead of waiting for me to make the first move.
❑ 6. Accept me as I am; accept me even when you see the worst side of me.

❑ 7. Tell me that you love me at times other than when we are in bed; phone sometimes just to say, "I love you!" Do not be ashamed to tell me, "I love you," in front of others.

❑ 8. While I am showering, find soft music on the radio.

❑ 9. Treat me as your wife, not as one of the children.

❑ 10. Honor Christ as the Head of the home.

❑ 11. Write love notes occasionally; send homemade love cards.

❑ 12. Talk to me after intercourse; make caresses after intercourse.

❑ 13. Be sweet and loving at least one hour before initiating sex.

❑ 14. Show an interest in what I have to say in the morning.

❑ 15. Do not seem as though you are bored with me in the evening.

❑ 16. Help me wash dinner dishes.

❑ 17. Go to bed at a decent hour, rather than watching television.

❑ 18. Say sweet little nothings and be silly.

❑ 19. Bring me a flower or candy occasionally, when you can afford to.

❑ 20. Occasionally buy me lingerie, perfume, and so forth.

❑ 21. Pay romantic attention to me (hold hands, kiss) even during relatively unromantic activities (watching television, riding in the car, etc.).

❑ 22. Help me feel that I am sexually and romantically attractive by complimenting me more often.

❑ 23. Tell me what you enjoy and when you are excited; express your desires more openly; share yourself more fully with me.

❑ 24. Try not to ejaculate so soon.

❑ 25. Express appreciation for the little things I have done that day.

❑ 26. Pray with me about the problems and victories you are having; let me express my own needs to you.

❑ 27. Appreciate the beauty of nature and share this appreciation with me.

❑ 28. Take more of the responsibility for getting the children settled so I can relax and share more of the evening with you.

❑ 29. Be patient with me; do not ridicule my slowness to reach orgasm.

❑ 30. Do not approach lovemaking as a ritualistic activity; make each time a new experience. Do not let lovemaking get boring by doing the same things over and over; try new things or new places.

❑ 31. Never try to make love with me when you are harboring bad feelings toward me or you know things are not right; let there be harmony between us so that sexual intercourse can indeed be an act of love.

❑ 32. Make me feel that I have worth as a person, warts and all!

❑ 33. Think of something nice to say about me in front of others occasionally.

❑ 34. Demonstrate agape love as well as eros.

❑ 35. Spend some quiet times with me, sharing life.

❑ 36. Other ideas: _____

_____

_____

Suggestions Husbands Have Made to Wives
  How to Make Sexual Relations More Meaningful

Husbands, read the following list and check those items you would like to mention to your wife.

❑ 1. Be attractive at bedtime. Wear something besides granny gowns and pajamas.

❑ 2. Be aggressive occasionally.

❑ 3. Be innovative and imaginative.

❑ 4. Do not be ashamed to show you are enjoying it.

❑ 5. Do not always be on a time schedule that places sex when we are both physically tired.

❑ 6. Dress more appealingly when I am at home.

❑ 7. Do things to catch my attention; man is easily excited by sight.

❑ 8. Communicate more openly about sex; communicate readiness for the actual act once foreplay has excited sufficiently.

❑ 9. Go to bed earlier.

❑ 10. Do not make me feel guilty at night for my inconsistencies during the day (not being affectionate enough, etc.).

❑ 11. Prolong the sexual relationship at times.

❑ 12. Be more aware of my needs and desires as a man.

❑ 13. Participate more fully and freely in the sexual act; be more submissive and open.

❑ 14. Allow variety in the time for the sexual act (not always at night).

❑ 15. Show more desire and understand that caressing and foreplay are as important to me as they are to you.

❑ 16. More varied positions; keep an open mind to variety.

❑ 17. Do not allow yourself to remain upset over everyday events that go wrong.

❑ 18. Relax together at least once a week.

Memorizing

Scripture

and

reviewing it

consistently

is a way

of getting

God's Word

into your

heart.

☐ 19. Stop trying to look romantic rather than being romantic.

☐ 20. Do not always play "hard to get."

☐ 21. Clear mind of daily things (today's and tomorrow's) and think about the matter on hand—love.

☐ 22. Do not say no too often.

☐ 23. Do not try to fake enjoyment.

☐ 24. Do not try to punish me by denying me sex or by giving it grudgingly.

☐ 25. Treat me like your lover.

☐ 26. Listen to my suggestions on what you can do to improve our sexual relationship.

☐ 27. Other ideas: _____

_____

_____

Assignments

1. When both of you have completed the above assignment, choose a time that will be free from interruptions and share with each other what you have checked. Discuss your thoughts and feelings about each subject. Concentrate on what your spouse is saying, rather than on trying to defend yourself. The purpose of your conversation is growth, not defense. Note here the date you had this sharing time. Date completed: _____

2. At another time, give personal thought to the things that your spouse shared, and note below some specific things you will seek to change to make the sexual experience more meaningful to your spouse.

Changes I want to make for the pleasure of my spouse:

(1) _____

(2) _____

(3) _____

3. Optional assignment: If you feel the need for additional information and suggestions in the area of sexual adjustment, you may want to read and discuss one or more of the following books.

- *The Gift of Sex* by Clifford and Joyce Penner (Word)
- *Sheet Music* by Kevin Leman (Tyndale)
- *Intended for Pleasure: New Approaches to Sexual Intimacy in Christian Marriage* by Ed Wheat, M.D. and Gaye Wheat (Revell)

All of these books are by Christian authors and give sound practical help in sexual growth. Open communication over the contents of these books will help you gain true sexual oneness.

SCRIPTURE MEMORY

1. Continue memorizing Luke 12:15. *"Then he said to them, 'Watch out! Be on your guard against all kinds of greed; a man's life does not consist in the abundance of his possessions'"* (Luke 12:15).

2. Memorizing Scripture and reviewing it consistently is a way of getting God's Word into your heart. As you review the six verses you have memorized in *A Couple's Guide to a Growing Marriage*, you will find many ways in which the truth contained in these verses will apply to your life. Remember, it is the Word applied to life that bears fruit.

3. Hopefully, you will select and memorize other verses of Scripture in the weeks ahead. Remember, however, it is better to memorize a few verses and consistently review them until they become a part of your life rather than memorize many verses and fail to review and apply them.

4. Write from memory the six verses you have memorized.

Ephesians 4:32: _____
_____

1 John 1:9: _____
_____

James 1:19: _____
_____

Philippians 2:3–4: _____
_____

Jeremiah 33:3: _____
_____

Luke 12:15: _____
_____

DAILY GROWTH EXERCISES

Conversations with God. Continue to record on page 129 the chapters you are reading, marking, and discussing with God each day.

The practice of meeting with God for a personal sharing time each day should be a regular part of the Christian's life. *A Couple's Guide to a Growing Marriage* has helped get you started in this practice. You will want to go on building your relationship with God by giving Him your undivided attention each day as you listen to His voice through the Scriptures. Then share with God what is on your heart.

Sharing Time with My Spouse. Continue to record on page 131 the days you have a sharing time with your spouse.

A daily sharing time with your spouse is essential to a growing marriage. When we stop sharing life, we stop growing. *A Couple's Guide to a Growing Marriage* has sought to help you establish this sharing time as a regular part of your marriage. You will want to continue this practice as the minimum daily requirement for a healthy relationship.

"Tell me three things that happened in your life today and how you felt about them" is a request designed to foster a shared life. If you practice sharing daily experiences, you will likely share deeper dreams, desires, joys, and sorrows. Remember, the purpose of communication is for getting to know and understand your spouse so that you can be a more effective minister to him or her. A commitment to discover and meet each other's needs is a commitment to growth.

Our prayer

is that you

and your

spouse have

made several

significant

discoveries

during the

past weeks.

ONLY THE BEGINNING

As we said in the introduction to *A Couple's Guide to a Growing Marriage*, this study can be a doorway to deeper relationships with God and your spouse. Our prayer is that you and your spouse have made several significant discoveries during the past weeks. Hopefully, you have gained insight into each other's needs and how those needs can be addressed. We trust that you have learned how to share your life more fully with God, and how to draw on His resources. Most important, we hope this study has been a doorway that you have traveled through. May what you find beyond the doorway challenge and equip you to develop deeper relationships with God and your spouse.

A Growing Marriage

In addition to his writing, Dr. Gary Chapman also leads a church-based, marriage enrichment seminar that provides Christian couples, engaged and married, biblical principles for marriage. In addition to a presentation of the five love languages, other topics include communication, decision-making, handling negative feelings, and making sex a mutual joy. These seminars are filled with humor and practical suggestions. They typically begin on Saturday morning and conclude on Saturday afternoon.

For more information, visit www.MoodyConferences.com or call (888) 824-8246.

My Conversations with God

One of the purposes of *A Couple's Guide to a Growing Marriage* is to help you establish a consistent daily time of listening and talking with God. This sheet is designed to encourage you to record the chapters from the Bible that you have read, marked, and discussed with God. List the book and chapter that you read each day.

My Sharing Times with My Spouse

A consistent, daily sharing time with your spouse is the mark of a growing marriage. This sheet will help you observe how well you are doing in establishing this time of communication. Write the date each day you and your spouse spend sharing with each other.

Be kind and compassionate to one another, forgiving each other, just as in Christ God forgave you.

EPHESIANS 4:32

If we confess our sins, he is faithful and just and will forgive us our sins and purify us from all unrighteousness.

1 JOHN 1:9

My dear brothers, take note of this: Everyone should be quick to listen, slow to speak and slow to become angry.

JAMES 1:19

Do nothing out of selfish ambition or vain conceit, but in humility consider others better than yourselves. Each of you should look not only to your own interests, but also to the interests of others. PHILIPPIANS 2:3–4

Call to me and I will answer you and tell you great and unsearchable things you do not know.

JEREMIAH 33:3

Then he said to them, "Watch out! Be on your guard against all kinds of greed; a man's life does not consist in the abundance of his possessions." LUKE 12:15

If we confess our sins, he is faithful and just and will forgive us our sins and purify us from all unrighteousness.

1 JOHN 1:9

Be kind and compassionate to one another, forgiving each other, just as in Christ God forgave you.

EPHESIANS 4:32

Do nothing out of selfish ambition or vain conceit, but in humility consider others better than yourselves. Each of you should look not only to your own interests, but also to the interests of others. PHILIPPIANS 2:3–4

My dear brothers, take note of this: Everyone should be quick to listen, slow to speak and slow to become angry.

JAMES 1:19

Then he said to them, "Watch out! Be on your guard against all kinds of greed; a man's life does not consist in the abundance of his possessions." LUKE 12:15

Call to me and I will answer you and tell you great and unsearchable things you do not know.

JEREMIAH 33:3

MY CONVERSATIONS WITH GOD

One of the purposes of *A Couple's Guide to a Growing Marriage* is to help you establish a consistent daily time of listening and talking with God. This sheet is designed to encourage you to record the chapters from the Bible that you have *read*, *marked*, and *discussed* with God. List the book and chapter that you read each day.

	SUN	MON	TUES	WED	THURS	FRI	SAT
WEEK ONE							
WEEK TWO							
WEEK THREE							
WEEK FOUR							
WEEK FIVE							
WEEK SIX							

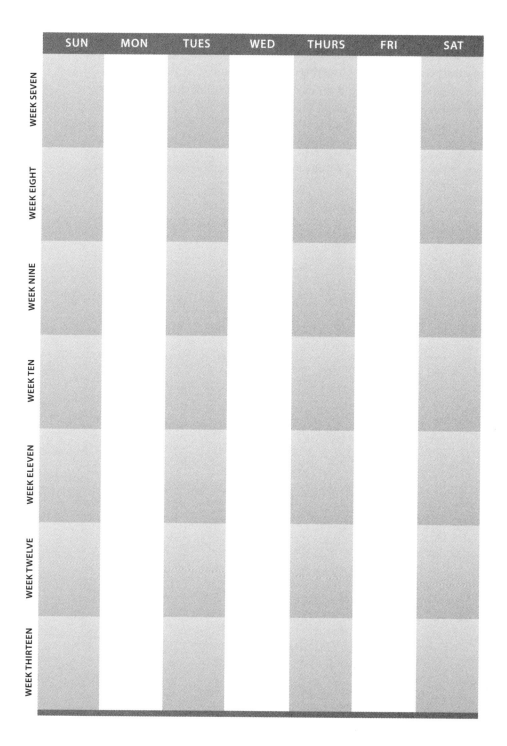

	SUN	MON	TUES	WED	THURS	FRI	SAT
WEEK SEVEN							
WEEK EIGHT							
WEEK NINE							
WEEK TEN							
WEEK ELEVEN							
WEEK TWELVE							
WEEK THIRTEEN							

MY SHARING TIMES WITH MY SPOUSE

A consistent, daily sharing time with your spouse is the mark of a growing marriage. This sheet will help you observe how well you are doing in establishing this time of communication. Write the date each day you and your spouse spend sharing time with each other.

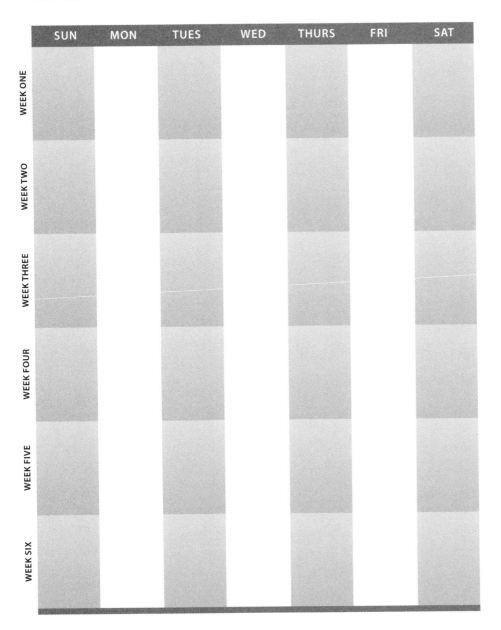

	SUN	MON	TUES	WED	THURS	FRI	SAT
WEEK ONE							
WEEK TWO							
WEEK THREE							
WEEK FOUR							
WEEK FIVE							
WEEK SIX							

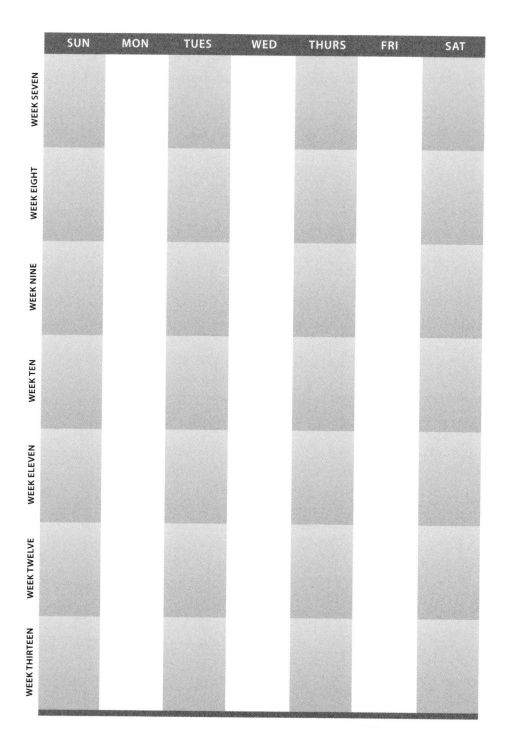

	SUN	MON	TUES	WED	THURS	FRI	SAT
WEEK SEVEN							
WEEK EIGHT							
WEEK NINE							
WEEK TEN							
WEEK ELEVEN							
WEEK TWELVE							
WEEK THIRTEEN							

RESOURCES

BUDGETING AND FINANCES

Blue, Ron with Jeremy White. *The New Master Your Money: A Step-by-Step Plan for Gaining and Enjoying Financial Freedom.* Chicago: Moody, 2004. Biblical guidance to earn, save, invest, and spend money wisely. Includes sections on the proper use of credit cards and making investments.

Burkett, Larry. *The Family Budget Workbook: Gaining Control of Your Personal Finances.* Chicago: Northfield, 2002. Through discussion and workbook forms this book gives the basics on financial planning and budgets. It contains forms for such items as budget analysis, short-range planning, and income and savings account allocations.

Dayton, Howard. *Free and Clear—God's Roadmap to Debt-Free Living.* Chicago: Moody, 2006. Practical advice on getting and staying out of debt.

Ramsey, Dave. *Financial Peace: Revisited.* New York: Viking, 2002. Covers the basics on budgeting, eliminating debt, systematic saving, and a proper lifestyle (living below your income). Chapters on money and marriage, money and your children, and money and your extended family and friends are especially helpful.

Internet resource: www.crown.org. This is the home page of Crown Financial Ministries, site of excellent resources ranging from books and radio programs to local seminars and guest speakers. CFM features the ministries of Christian Financial Concepts and Crown Ministries.

CONFLICT AND COMMUNICATION

Chapman, Gary. *The Other Side of Love: Handling Anger in a Godly Way.* Chicago: Moody, 1999. Anger is a misunderstood emotion that goes hand-in-hand with love. Its fundamental purpose is not to tear down, but to motivate us to positive, loving action that will leave things better than we found them.

Cloud, Henry and John Townsend. *Boundaries in Marriage.* Grand Rapids: Zondervan, 2002. Knowing and respecting each other's needs, choices, and freedom will enable couples to give themselves freely and lovingly to one another in marriage. Setting boundaries will allow couples to move beyond friction points to the mutual care, respect, affirmation, and intimacy they both long for.

Downs, Tim and Joy Downs. *Fight Fair: Winning at Conflict Without Losing at Love.* Chicago: Moody, 2003. Conflict is "the art of disagreeing while still holding hands," and the authors remind every married couple that conflict is a part of marriage and of life that they cannot escape. Learn to play by the rules, and tensions can be redirected for the good of your marriage. Readers learn to establish their own rules of engagement and to employ the appropriate underlying attitudes, which include humility, generosity, and gentleness. Tim's hilarious cartoons are a welcome bonus.

Downs, Tim and Joy Downs. *The Seven Conflicts: Resolving the Most Common Disagreements in Marriage.* Chicago: Moody, 2003. This companion book to *Fight Fair* presents the seven areas where most conflicts occur and prescribes how to resolve each conflict when alienation has set in. The seven areas, which reflect differences in male and female approaches to issues, are security, loyalty, responsibility, caring, order, openness, and connection (how we communicate and make decisions).

Farrel, Bill and Pam Farrel. *Men Are Like Waffles, Women Are Like Spaghetti.* Eugene, Oreg.: Harvest, 2001. The differences between men and women, popularized in John Gray's *Men Are from Mars, Women Are from Venus*, are brought down to earth in this funny, practical book on gender differences that lead to misunderstanding and conflict. Practical guidelines abound.

Special resource: Chapman, Gary and Ramon Presson. *Love Talks.* Chicago: Northfield, 2002. Sometimes a wife really doesn't know her husband; sometimes a husband knows only the surface of his mate, not what "makes her tick." More than one hundred questions are listed in a fun flip chart to help couples disclose and discover, both key elements to creating or restoring intimacy in marriage.

PERSONAL INTIMACY

Benner, David G. *Sacred Companions.* Downers Grove, Ill.: InterVarsity, 2002. The author informs about the benefits and ways to develop spiritual friendship and spiritual direction, including in the context of small groups and marriage.

Harley Jr., Willard F. *His Needs, Her Needs.* Grand Rapids: Revell, 2001. Men and women have ten identical needs for a marriage relationship that sustains romance and builds intimacy. However, the top needs for husbands differ from those of wives. Harley helps spouses understand those differences and express love to their mates.

McGinnis, Alan Loy. *The Friendship Factor.* Minneapolis: Augsburg, 2004. This book is a must for couples who want to become friends. It is filled with ideas on how to deepen relationships, cultivate intimacy, handle negative emotions, and forgive.

Snyder, Chuck and Barb Snyder. *Incompatibility: Still Grounds for a Great Marriage.* Sisters, Oreg.: Multnomah, 1999. People often feel that differences in marriage are simply to be endured or eliminated. Discover how to truly accept and enjoy each other's personalities. Find out how your differences can actually help strengthen your relationship.

TerKeurst, Lysa. *Capture His Heart* and *Capture Her Heart.* Chicago: Moody, both 2002. Since men and women are different in their needs and expectations, husbands and wives often miss the mark in helping their mates. *Capture His Heart,* written for a wife, shows how she can build up her husband's confidence and strength emotionally, vocationally, and relationally; *Capture Her Heart,* written for a husband, explains how he can be the lover, leader, and confidant his wife wants him to be.

Internet resource and magazine: www.christianitytoday.com/marriage. This Web site contains practical articles with a wholly biblical viewpoint on marriage from the pages of *Marriage Partnership.* The quarterly magazine is available for subscription through the Web site.

SEXUAL INTIMACY

Leman, Kevin. *Sheet Music.* Wheaton: Tyndale, 2003. With typical candor, Leman tells couples everything they need to know about having great sex. From healthy and loving attitudes to fun and creative positions, Leman helps couples know how to make sex as fulfilling as God intended it to be. Not only will you come away with exciting insight and practical suggestions; you'll laugh out loud and find it difficult to put this book down.

Penner, Clifford and Joyce Penner. *The Gift of Sex.* Nashville: W Publishing, 2003. One of the most comprehensive and practical guides to discovering mutual sexual fulfillment in a marriage. The book deals realistically with common struggles and frustrations. It speaks to the most often asked questions of couples who want to find sexual harmony. For couples who want answers, this book is priceless.

Penner, Clifford and Joyce Penner. *The Married Guy's Guide to Great Sex.* Wheaton: Tyndale, 2004. This book is written specifically for husbands. The Penners talk candidly about the things that make the difference between average, going-through-the-motions routine and a passionate, exciting love life that meets the needs of both husband and wife.

Rosenau, Douglas and Childerston, Jim and Carolyn. *A Celebration of Sex After 50.* Nashville: Nelson, 2004. True to its title, this book emphasizes that sex after age fifty is indeed something to celebrate! Though bodies change and desires may fluctuate, couples can ignite passion in many creative and mutually satisfying ways. Plain-spoken and compassionate, the authors confront issues many couples hesitate to bring up—then offer frank, detailed answers.

ONENESS IN MARRIAGE

Dobson, James. *Love for a Lifetime.* Bend, Oreg.: Multnomah, 1999. Ideal for young couples contemplating or beginning marriage.

Mason, Mike. *The Mystery of Marriage.* Bend, Oreg.: Multnomah, 2001. An inspiring search for understanding of the wondrous dynamics of committed love. Chapters include "Otherness," "Vows," "Intimacy," "Sex," and "Submission."

Thomas, Gary. *Sacred Marriage.* Grand Rapids: Zondervan, 2002. God's primary intent for your marriage is not to make you happy; it's to make you holy. The author looks at how God uses marriage to teach us respect, develop our prayer life, reveal our sins, build perseverance, develop a forgiving spirit, and much more.

Wangerin Jr., Walter. *As for Me and My House.* Nashville: Nelson, 2001. The centerpiece of marriage is not love but forgiveness. Through transparent recounting of his own failings in the marriage relationship, the author reveals the healing power of forgiveness. A master storyteller, Wangerin offers personal stories that will reveal, convict, and inspire readers in their own marriages.

Young, Ed. *The Ten Commandments of Marriage.* Chicago: Moody, 2003. Marriage is to be a lifelong covenant, but both newlyweds and those married many years fall into bad habits that can cripple a marriage. Using humor and stories of successes and failures from his own marriage, the author looks at ten ways to rejuvenate a marriage. The "commandments," all based on Scripture, include communicating, forgiving, making conflict your ally, fleeing sexual temptation, and building a winning team.

DEVOTIONAL

Dobson, James and Shirley. *Night Light.* Sisters, Oreg: Multnomah, 2000. Daily devotions for couples covering twenty-six weekly themes. Includes Scripture references, questions, prayers, brief commentary.

Eldridge, John. *The Ransomed Heart.* Nashville: Nelson, 2005. A year's worth of daily devotions featuring excerpts from Eldridge's books.

Ferguson, David and Teresa. *One Year Book of Devotions for Couples.* Wheaton: Tyndale, 2004. Daily devotions offering a Scripture verse, meditation, prayer, commitment questions.

Omartian, Stormie. *The Power of a Praying Husband.* Eugene, Oreg.: Harvest House, 2001. Short chapters on praying for aspects of a wife's needs such as her priorities, purpose, work, spirit. Gives sample prayers and Scripture references.

Omartian, Stormie. *The Power of a Praying Wife.* Eugene, Oreg.: Harvest House, 1997. Short chapters on praying for aspects of a husband's needs such as his mind, affections, temptations, relationships. Gives sample prayers and Scripture references.

Quiet Moments with God for Couples. Colorado Springs: Honor Books, 2002.

Spangler, Ann. *Praying the Names of God—A Daily Guide.* Grand Rapids: Zondervan, 2004. A fresh and interesting devotional, exploring Hebrew names of God. Offers one name per week for twenty-six weeks, with a daily meditation and suggestions on praying using God's various names.

GENERAL

Chapman, Gary. *The Four Seasons of a Marriage.* Wheaton: Tyndale, 2005. Marriages go through recurring seasons, no matter how long a couple has been married. A fresh approach to understanding different times in a marriage.

Jenkins, Jerry. *Hedges: Loving Your Marriage Enough to Protect It.* Wheaton: Crossway, 2005. Real-life stories of how small things can creep into a marriage and cause it to crumble. Encouragement on being watchful to take care of your marriage.

Visit www.GaryChapman.org for a schedule of Dr. Chapman's marriage conferences or to receive a daily e-mail from Dr. Chapman on practical ideas for stimulating marital growth.

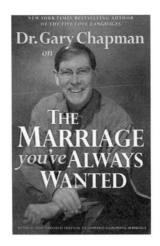

DR. GARY CHAPMAN ON
THE MARRIAGE YOU'VE ALWAYS WANTED

How does a couple "become one"—whatever their stage of marriage? And what are some of the issues that block that oneness? With the practical encouragement that has made him a best-selling relationship expert, Gary Chapman looks at such challenges as open communication, sexual fulfillment, money management, dealing with extended family, and much more.

ISBN 0-8024-8786-6

LOVING SOLUTIONS

Are you living in a seriously flawed marriage? Gary Chapman offers hope. Discover practical and permanent solutions and take positive steps to change your marriage. Recipient of the Gold Medallion Book Award.

ISBN 1-881273-91-1

more resources from

GARY CHAPMAN

speak more fluently, love more deeply

PARENTING YOUR ADULT CHILD

Few resources are available to help parents communicate with their child who is no longer a child. Here's a tool that will help you deal with such issues as: Helping Your Child Find Success, When Adult Children Return with Their Children, and more.

ISBN 1-881273-12-1

LOVE TALKS FOR FAMILIES

One of the signs of a healthy family is open and meaningful communication. But how do you find something the whole family can talk about together? *Love Talks* gives you 101 questions to facilitate this process in a convenient, spiral-bound booklet.

ISBN 1-881273-49-0

Also available:

Love Talks for Couples
ISBN 1-881273-48-2

More Love Talks for Couples
ISBN 1-881273-50-4

THE FIVE LOVE LANGUAGES

We all want to love and be loved. But how can we learn to express that love—especially to our mate? By learning his or her "love language," says Dr. Gary Chapman. It's a message that's positive, hopeful, and easy to apply—as more than 3 million readers have already discovered.

ISBN 1-881273-15-6

Audio Cassette ISBN 1-881273-56-3

CD Version ISBN 1-881273-37-7

more resources on

THE FIVE LOVE LANGUAGES

speak more fluently, love more deeply

THE FIVE LOVE LANGUAGES JOURNAL

Now you can journalize your thoughts, feelings, and progress on keeping your mate's love tank full with *The Five Love Languages Journal*. Use the entries to spark communication or keep them as a private retreat. Duotone faux-leather will appeal to both men and women.

ISBN 1-881273-71-7

THE FIVE LOVE LANGUAGES MEN'S EDITION

Men: How can you learn to speak (and understand) the love language of the woman in your life? This special edition of the bestselling *The Five Love Languages* includes new features just for men! Complete the profile and discover her and your love languages . . . then try out some of the new end-of-chapter ideas on showing heartfelt love to that special woman in your life.

ISBN 1-881273-10-5

THE FIVE LOVE LANGUAGES OF CHILDREN

Kids desperately need to know they are loved. Dr. Gary Chapman teams with physician Ross Campbell, bestselling author of *How to Really Love Your Child*, to show you how to speak your child's love language . . . fluently!

ISBN 1-881273-65-2

Audio Cassette ISBN 1-881273-11-3

CD Version ISBN 1-881273-85-7

more resources on

THE FIVE LOVE LANGUAGES

speak more fluently, love more deeply

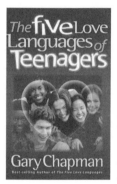

THE FIVE LOVE LANGUAGES OF TEENAGERS

It's tough to raise teens—today more than ever. Yet, says bestselling author Dr. Gary Chapman, parents, not peers, are the strongest influence on their teens. And the door to that influence is love. Using his famed five love languages principles, Dr. Chapman shares real stories and expert wisdom to encourage you as you rear—and love—your teen.

ISBN 1-881273-39-3

Audio Cassette ISBN 1-881273-31-8

CD Version ISBN 1-881273-78-4

THE FIVE LOVE LANGUAGES FOR SINGLES

Single adults have unique needs—yet they, like everyone, also need to give love and be loved. Chapman looks at the special joys and challenges singles face, and helps them apply the five love languages to their lives—at work, in relationships, and more.

ISBN 1-881273-98-9

CD Version ISBN 1-881273-52-0

THE OTHER SIDE OF LOVE

Many of us need help with anger. But can anger be used for good? Yes, says Dr. Gary Chapman, who shows us how we can move anger "from one side to another"—toward love.

ISBN 0-8024-6777-6

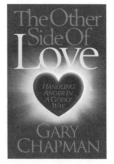

more resources on

THE FIVE LOVE LANGUAGES

speak more fluently, love more deeply

THE LOVE LANGUAGES OF GOD

Did you know that each of us has our own unique spiritual love language that helps us connect with God? How can you discover your primary love language . . . and learn new "dialects" to deepen your spiritual journey and strengthen your love for God? Learn how to apply the bestselling principles of the five love languages to your own spiritual life.

ISBN 1-881273-93-8

FIVE SIGNS OF A LOVING FAMILY

In modern Western culture, it is widely acknowledged that the family is in serious trouble. Despite the odds, you desire is to have family relationships that are fully loving and functional. If you want to establish healthy patterns in your own family, you'll need to learn how to recognize and apply the qualities they share.

ISBN 1-881273-92-X